D1458286

WHY VOTE UKIP 2015

WHY V**O**TE UKIP

2015

UKIP

SUZANNE EVANS

Biteback Publishing

First published in Great Britain in 2014 by
Biteback Publishing Ltd
Westminster Tower
3 Albert Embankment
London SE1 7SP
Copyright © Suzanne Evans 2014

ISBN 978-1-84954-737-6

10 9 8 7 6 5 4 3 2 1

A CIP catalogue record for this book is available from the British Library.

Set in Chaparral Pro

Printed and bound in Great Britain by
CPI Group (UK) Ltd, Croydon CR0 4YY

MIX
Paper from
responsible sources
FSC® C020471
www.fsc.org

For Richard

Contents

Introduction:
Why Not Vote UKIP?

Why vote UKIP? Perhaps the first question we should ask is why would you NOT vote UKIP?

Unless you are already a staunch UKIP supporter, your reply to this question is likely to be either 'because I firmly believe we should stay in Europe' or something along the lines of 'because I could never vote for a sexist/racist/homophobic/isolationist/fruitcake party like UKIP'.

To be honest, if everything written in the press or in other political parties' literature about UKIP was true, then I would not be voting UKIP either, let alone supporting the party and standing for election under the UKIP banner. I am a woman. I have spent most of my life working with, supporting and promoting ethnic minority and multi-faith communities. I travel frequently in Europe as the founder of a national health charity which values and thrives on its links with like-minded organisations across the continent where research and treatments are far more advanced than here in Britain. And oddly enough, I was persuaded to join this 'homophobic' party by a gay friend and colleague.

I did take quite some persuading; it was not a decision I made lightly. At the time I was a disillusioned Conservative councillor in the London Borough of Merton. Under David Cameron's leadership it seemed to me the Conservative Party had abandoned long-held principles of aspiration, fairness and equality of opportunity. The 2010 Tory manifesto was either torn up in places or reinterpreted in ways one might never have expected, while bewildering and unpopular legislation was being drafted in the face of opposition from party members. It was becoming harder and harder to justify being a Conservative on the doorstep out canvassing and I found myself in the unenviable position of agreeing with most of our detractors. I had also become deeply cynical about local government, seeing spiteful politicking, extravagant waste and a lack of accountability or real democracy within my (Labour-run) council. There was also a distinct lack of talent among some councillors who were making major decisions on constituents' behalf, and I saw a good deal of what I considered to be unethical behaviour. It was not a pretty spectacle.

Is it any wonder disillusionment within politics is rife, I wondered? I could understand why so many people – often the majority in some elections – had stopped voting altogether. My first instinct was to give up myself and be shot of the whole charade. But, being made of stronger stuff and fuelled by my colleague's enthusiasm, I looked into what UKIP really believed, as opposed to what others unconnected to the party claimed it believed, and found I could agree with most of UKIP's core principles. I met or spoke with leading figures in the party – Nigel Farage himself got on the phone – and the rest is my personal history still in the making.

The question now is: can I now convince you?

You will make your own decision. My job in writing this book is to give you the tools to do so, to put the record straight and set out what UKIP *really* stands for, so you *can* make your own, informed choice at the ballot box, and not a choice informed by the prejudice of our detractors. I've lost count of the amount of times a 'UKIP policy' has been announced on the radio, TV or in the papers, on social media or in other parties' campaign literature when UKIP does not have any such policy. 'UKIP wants to privatise the NHS' is probably Labour's favourite, while the Lib Dems prefer to chant the false mantra that 'UKIP's policies will cost us three million jobs in Europe.'

These smears are at the tame end, of course. You would have to have been living the life of a hermit to have missed the hardcore slurs from what UKIP supporters often refer to in shorthand as the 'LibLabCon', the other main political parties, their spin doctors and their media luvvies in the national press who have traditionally always come down on either the left or the right as opposed to what I now know is UKIP's common-sense centre. While ignoring criminal behaviour in their own ranks (I write this at the beginning of the Westminster child abuse scandal), the old parties' apparatchiks troll through UKIP candidates' Twitter and Facebook accounts to drag up unsavoury remarks often made years previously, or take an off-the-cuff 'joke' a little bit too seriously and find someone to be 'offended' by it. They then phone the national press, which pounces on the 'story' and decides it is of such great national importance it should be run on the front pages or at the top of news bulletins, even though the same script would barely be worth a mention in the local paper if it was a Labour, Tory or Lib Dem party member who was implicated.[1]

The classic example of this was the 'gay floods' row, when comments made by a town councillor suggested gay marriage legislation was to blame for recent flooding. Bonkers? Unacceptable? Yes, both, but nothing new for him. He had been saying much the same for years as a Conservative councillor and no one had taken a blind bit of notice. Suddenly, when he joined UKIP, he achieved national fame and seized the headlines for days. Staggeringly, the government even sent ministers – yes, ministers – onto our TV screens to condemn his folly. Clearly there was no real governance to be done that week.

There are few insults that have not been thrown at UKIP. My personal favourite is the at least fairly humorous jibe that UKIP is 'the *Dad's Army* of politics'. Well, as Lance Corporal Jones said, that is only because 'they don't like it up 'em'.

---

1   In just one week in April 2014, seventeen Labour, Tory or Liberal Democrat councillors were arrested, charged or convicted for crimes including perverting the course of justice, child pornography, firearms and electoral fraud. In the same period, a further thirteen were involved in racism, sexism or homophobic scandals. Only one, in which Lord Hanningfield was jailed for expenses fraud, featured in the national media.

UKIP is twenty-one years old this year. It has come of age. We won the 2014 European elections, taking twenty-four MEP seats, more than any other political party. We have come second in numerous recent parliamentary by-elections, forcing the other parties to throw everything they have into defending what should be safe seats in need of little campaign funds or energy. UKIP now has 284 District, County and Borough councillors across the country, plus numerous Parish councillors taking 'on your doorstep' decisions day in, day out. We have built up solid levels of support in many English constituencies and are set to enter parliament for the first time in 2015 – at the time of writing, it looks as if the former Conservative MP Douglas Carswell may well even get there sooner and become UKIP's first elected MP ahead of the general election. The three old parties' cages are being well and truly rattled by UKIP. They are terrified of losing control of the cosy cartel they have been running for decades and, being tribal politicians, won't stop at much to maintain their hold on power. UKIP's grassroots success has brought out the worst in the political elite who presently run Britain. Instead of listening to the discontent, and taking action, they continue the Punch and Judy show, regularly playing the man and not the ball. They should be ashamed by the lies they tell to smear UKIP and the tactics they use to keep control.

However, voters genuinely concerned about immigration, and for good reason, do not like to be told they are racist by the out-of-touch and the over-privileged, or by the London-centric liberal media. UKIP is taking millions of votes from the old parties and, significantly, getting votes from many who have never voted before, or who have not felt confident enough to vote for a very long time. Why? Because people see in UKIP a political party that at last speaks for them, instead of at them, one that offers a fresh choice for Britain.

Traditional working-class Labour voters are turning to UKIP because they have woken up to the fact that the Labour party sold out on the working man and woman long ago, cutting the 10p tax

rate and throwing open our borders to migrant workers looking for
their minimum wage jobs but prepared to work for even less. They
also recognise that today's Labour Party has all but completely lost
sight of its working class roots. Most Labour MPs are now indistinguishable from those on the Tory benches – millionaire, privately
educated Oxbridge graduates whose only jobs have been in politics. Ed Miliband, like David Cameron, worked as a parliamentary
researcher and advisor before becoming an MP. In 1979, 40 per cent
of Labour MPs had done manual labour or clerical work at some point
in their careers. By 2010 that figure had fallen to just 9 per cent and
now about half of all Labour candidates selected to fight winnable
seats at the general election already have links to Westminster as
former special advisors, parliamentary researchers or lobbyists, or
they have been employed by the party.[2]

The political class reproduces itself: is it any wonder we get fed
up with career politicians who all look and sound the same? UKIP's
Deputy Leader, Paul Nuttall MEP, spoke for many Labour voters
when he said in his speech to the UKIP Conference in 2013: 'Labour
MPs today wouldn't know what it's like in a working men's club and
wouldn't know a council estate if it fell out of the sky and hit them
on the head.'

Having forgotten those whom they once pledged to represent,
Labour MPs have become indistinguishable from the wealthy met-
ropolitan elite who embrace open-door migration because of the
benefits it gives them in terms of access to cheap nannies, house-
keepers, chauffeurs and cleaners, while suffering none of the social
problems brought by immigration. They, after all, can afford their
own private healthcare, private education for their children and
don't have to worry about the cost of petrol or the downsides of spiralling house prices. Meanwhile, the real British working classes are
suffering; there are now a million fewer low-skilled British workers

---

2   Research by former Labour Cabinet minister, Peter Hain.

in jobs than there were when the last Labour government came to power in 1997,[3] and many low-skilled workers now find it impossible to even get on the social housing waiting list, such is the strain on resources. Labour's attempts to play to their old core vote seem limited to puerile class war insults cast across the debating chamber. No wonder then that former Labour voters are deserting the party in droves, so out of touch with their needs, hopes and dreams are its current representatives.

Meanwhile, the middle classes turn to UKIP because the Conservatives too are out of touch. They might talk about 'strivers' and 'hard-working families' but these are just meaningless soundbites. The Tories have not looked after these people. The cost of living crisis has hit the middle classes hard.

Those on middle incomes have seen take-home pay cut since Chancellor George Osborne lowered the 40 per cent tax threshold and they are pushed into it. VAT (an EU tax) is at its highest rate ever in the UK, making both small luxuries and major purchases unaffordable. Energy bills continue to soar as Cameron pursues a flawed energy policy, bowing down to European Union directives and refusing to cut the 'green taxes' that add hundreds of pounds to our fuel bills every year. Healthcare and education may well still be free, but getting a doctor's appointment can be a mammoth task and the local school can't always be trusted to deliver a good education for all manner of reasons. Work hard, earn good money, and it is still tough getting a foot on the property ladder.

Shockingly, the Conservatives no longer seem to want to give everyone a chance to 'better themselves', to use a rather old-fashioned phrase. Despite the fact 66 per cent of Conservative voters want grammar schools,[4] the Tories refuse to bring them back to help bright children from poorer backgrounds. Worse, they have

---

3   Migration Advisory Committee report on the growth of European Union (EU) and non-EU labour in low-skilled jobs and its impact on the UK, published 8 July 2014.

4   YouGov poll of Greater London residents in June 2013.

actively prevented new grammar schools from opening even where current legislation allows it. Even when young adults from average backgrounds do get good qualifications, they either can't find jobs, or their ambitions to move into higher education are stymied. The huge hike in university tuition fees – pushed through when the Lib Dems infamously reneged on their famous manifesto pledge – was, for many Tory voters, the final straw. The children of the wealthy, or those confident they will get highly paid jobs in the future, will no doubt have no hesitation in attending university still, but what of those without such fiscal or occupational confidence? Far from being the party of aspiration and social mobility, it could be argued the Tories today are rapidly winning a reputation as the party of defenestrated life chances.

Then, of course, there is the culture of entitlement that has been bred at Westminster, the symptoms of which have manifested themselves in a succession of parliamentary humiliations, most notably, perhaps, the 2009 expenses scandal, when few MPs were *not* caught fleecing the taxpayer in all manner of senseless and inventive ways. Parliament should be a noble place, where injustice is put right and good deeds done; instead, a shroud of disrespect has been cast over it, as members let themselves and the country down by mis-behaviour. We sense that politicians are only 'in it for themselves', a commonplace phrase. We become frustrated at their fearful ina-bility to speak their minds, let alone the truth, and this contrasts with their competence at delivering flat, politically correct plati-tudes and soundbites.

Take all this into account and it's not difficult to see why UKIP is on the rise, especially with the highly charismatic, expressive and straight-talking Nigel Farage MEP at the helm. Currently the only political party leader who has a positive personal rating in public opinion polls,[5] Nigel's forthright ability to 'tell it as it is' is a refreshing

---

5   YouGov survey for the *Sunday Times*, 15–16 May 2014.

antidote to the current bunch of MPs who come across as being increasingly out of touch and less trustworthy. It is hardly surprising that UKIP is now the only practical, mainstream alternative to this deeply unsatisfactory status quo.

Precisely because of this, however, some denounce UKIP votes as 'protest votes'. Actually, this is yet another insult to the electorate from those in the Westminster bubble. In any case, from what I have seen at election time, 'protest votes' get counted in exactly the same way as any others.

But yes, the general idea in British politics is that we should vote *for* a particular party or candidate, and not *against* others. So, as disillusioned with traditional three-party politics and politicians as any one of us may be, any decent party or candidate would hope that we would vote for them because we believe in what they stand for and not only because we are unconvinced by their opponents.

If you believe it should be the MPs we elect who make our laws, not unelected foreign bureaucrats; if you want to be able to trade freely with Europe but not be bound into political union with our European neighbours; and if you want independence from the ever-deepening clutches of undue government interference, your vote should go to UKIP. If you are in favour of fairer taxes and lower fuel bills; agree we *should* be talking about the problems caused by mass uncontrolled immigration; consider the law of the land should apply equally to all; and agree politicians should be the servants of the people and not the other way around, then putting a cross in the box next to the UKIP logo on your 2015 general election ballot paper is the only sensible option.

One of the main reasons I stand with UKIP is because I love my country. I'm no fanatical patriot but I do think it is about time parliament recovered power over our national life, started putting Britain first again and made a fundamental commitment to stand up for Britain and the British people. This is surely the only reason our MPs have been elected, and the only reason we have a parliament? So why do so many shy away from protecting British values and institutions, and seem almost embarrassed to talk about patriotism?

UKIP isn't embarrassed by patriotism or by being British. We believe our nation can be a force for good and that our country has developed social and civic values over the last thousand years which should be celebrated, preserved and built upon. This is the philosophy at the heart of all UKIP policies and one which underlies all our principles. Many UKIP voters tell me they feel 'our British way of life is under threat' or they say: 'We want our country back.' While we cannot and should not turn back the clock – it certainly isn't UKIP's aim to take the country back to the '50s, as our critics have suggested – we do believe the British way of life is fundamentally good and worth saving. This is why our foremost policy is withdrawal from the European Union.

Perhaps though, you are one of those put off voting UKIP because of this fundamental policy? Again, this is an area that has been much misunderstood. Frequently we hear in the media that UKIP is 'anti-Europe'. This is rubbish, pure and simple. UKIP is certainly not anti-Europe, but is it vehemently opposed to the political federation that is the European Union.

Britain was once a proud, independent, sovereign nation. Since we joined the European Union in 1973, successive Labour and Conservative governments have, step by stealthy step, signed away our sovereignty and independence. Originally we were told – with astonishing duplicity – that we were entering a 'common market', as it was then called. This is all most of us ever wanted. What we have ended up with is a diminishing role in a pan-European super-state that has its own flag, its own national anthem, its own parliament, its own military force, and a small, unelected, undemocratic commission working solely to impose new regulations and directives on us and other member states. Our hands are now tied in so many ways: we are no longer allowed even make our own trade deals, not even with Commonwealth countries, despite our still strong ties. Now, the EU negotiates international trade deals on our behalf. Joining the European 'common market' has prevented us from trading with the rest of the world on our own terms. Once the strongest trading nation on the planet, we now play a greatly reduced role in global commerce.

Have you ever noticed that the two main issues national politicians argue over are the NHS and education? This isn't just because they are issues that tear at the heartstrings and sway voters, but also because they are two of very few policy areas left to fight over at election time. Control of just about everything else has either, wholly or in part, been relinquished to the EU. The EU controls financial services, fishing, farming, energy and trade. It dictates business and employment legislation as well as immigration rules. It seeks greater control over law and order, foreign affairs and tax. There is momentum behind plans for an EU-wide army and police force. The EU 'shares' responsibility with us for many other policy areas too – animal welfare, consumer protection, public health, space programmes, social policy, humanitarian aid and vocational training, to mention but a few. Rarely does the EU fail to poke its nose somewhere in British legislature.

Is this what you really want when you say you want to 'stay in Europe'? Or do you just want to be able to trade openly and freely with businesses on the Continent?

And what of the EU edict that has had the biggest impact on Britain, the one that is most talked about and resented, the one which insists on the free movement of people across EU member state borders? This, combined with the former Labour government's deliberate policy to 'engineer multiculturalism' by purposely letting immigration spiral out of control – even sending out 'search parties' for migrants between 1997 and 2010[6] – has changed the social

---

6   Peter Mandelson's admission in a speech to a rally organised by think tank Progress as reported in the *Daily Mail*, 14 May 2013.

and physical landscape of Britain beyond recognition in some parts of the country. Today, one in seven UK residents was born outside Britain; in London that figure rises to one in three. There are now eight million immigrants living in the UK.[7] It is a situation that concerns the vast majority of people in Britain, including those from ethnic minority groups.[8]

In 1973, we joined a common market with others of a similar economic status. There was no great desire or need back then for low-skilled workers in these countries to migrate to find work. Now, the EU has expanded to comprise twenty-eight member states in total, including many desperately poor, former communist countries from Southern Europe, with more to come. Quite understandably, many people living in these countries want to come to Britain to find a better way of life. In the last decade, over 2.5 million people have arrived in Britain in total from all EU member states.

The strain this puts on public services such as schools, hospitals and local housing provisions is immense, yet our current politicians lack the desire, the determination and the means to do much about it. As far as jobs are concerned, the trade unions who are supposed to stand up for British working people and protect their jobs are instead reported to be selling cut-price memberships to Romanian and Bulgarian migrants and giving them free advice on how to claim benefits in the UK.[9]

Until we leave the EU and take back control of our borders it remains theoretically possible for almost 500 million residents in other EU member states to take up residence in Britain and take advantage of all the benefits our country has to offer.

Meanwhile, we are unable to deport foreign criminals from anywhere in the world because of our compulsory surrender to the

---

7   Figures from the Office for National Statistics.
8   'Briefing from the Migration Observatory on UK Public Opinion toward Immigration: Overall Attitudes and Level of Concern' by Dr Scott Blinder, published 3 July 2014.
9   'Romanians and Bulgarians taught how to claim UK benefits in return for joining union', *Daily Mail*, 13 December 2013.

judgements of the European Court of Human Rights. We are forced
to dump fish worth £130 million as a result of the Common Fisheries Policy.[10] Our welfare bill soars as the European Court of Human
Rights rules we must pay benefits to all EU migrants, irrespective of
whether they have ever paid into the system or even intend to work.
We are required to build EU-driven vanity projects we can't afford,
such as the HS2 rail link. The list goes on and on.

It would be bad enough that we face all these problems; worse still
is the fact we pay a fortune for them. To suffer the consequences of
uncontrollable mass immigration, to abdicate our sovereignty and
to invite a plethora of burdensome interference in our laws, our
democracy and our business dealings, we hand over astonishingly
high membership fees to the EU of some £55 million *every day*. We
get some of that back, but less than half, by anyone's analysis.[11]
We are currently the EU's second highest net contributor after
Germany. According to economist Professor Tim Congdon, the
cost of our EU membership, plus the cost of complying with EU
regulations, comes to around £150 billion annually, or 11 per cent
of GDP.[12] This is without taking into account the £25 billion or so
we have paid towards bailing out failing Euro countries such as
Ireland and Greece.

The next time you see the words 'funded by the EU' on a smart
new public building, publication or charity website, stop and think:
whose money has really funded this? The answer is simple: yours.

UKIP's perspective is equally simple: change. We cannot afford
to carry on like this, not financially, not practically, not socially. We
would be better off out of the EU.

Out of the EU we can make our own trade deals with other

---

10 Figure courtesy of the TaxPayers' Alliance.
11 According to the Office for Budget Responsibility and HM Treasury, for instance, in
    2012 the UK paid the EU more than £12 billion (excluding the rebate of approximately
    £3 billion) and received around £4 billion back in EU spending on Britain.
12 *How Much Does the EU Cost Britain?* by Professor Tim Condon, published by the UK
    Independence Party, 2013.

nations, as Switzerland and Norway do with great success – they are the fourth and fifth largest non-member state exporters to the EU respectively after China, Russia and the USA; although geographically within Europe, they are free from the shackles of EU membership. Out of the EU we can decide who comes to live here not on the basis of their last country of residence, but what they have to offer Britain. We can choose our new citizens on an equal and non-racist basis from the entire world population, whatever their colour or creed and not because we must give unfettered priority to those from the predominantly white, Christian EU. We can take positive steps to cut UK unemployment by advertising British jobs in Britain instead of advertising them right across Europe as we are obliged to do at the moment. We can take back control of our borders, take back control of our laws and take back control of our heritage and culture. Then, and only then, might we get at least some of our country back.

In a nutshell, UKIP, for me, is a patriotic party with common-sense solutions to Britain's problems. Those who think we are a 'single-issue party' are shamefully out of date. We have fully costed, sound and reasonable solutions to the economic crisis, the employment crisis and our energy crisis. Our forthcoming manifesto will reveal solutions to the problems caused by uncontrolled mass immigration and the rising burden it puts on our social services. We have a fresh vision for education, welfare, healthcare and care for the elderly. We want to transform foreign affairs and foreign aid in a way that protects our own national security. We want to take back responsibility for agriculture and fishing.

Perhaps most importantly of all though, we want to re-engage the British public in politics through direct democracy. We want to see a smaller, less intrusive government that gives the British people a genuine and binding say in the key issues of the day through national and local referenda. UKIP doesn't see a government as ruling over the people of Britain, but as being in partnership with them.

Recent European and local elections have proven that, at last, if you vote UKIP, you get UKIP. We are ready for power. Are you ready to vote for us and take power with us?

Chapter 1

Leaving the European Union

A vote for UKIP is a vote to remove the United Kingdom from the unaccountable supranational government of the European Union and re-establish Britain as an independent, influential power on the world stage.

In May 2014, when the people of Britain voted in the European Parliament elections, UKIP topped the poll and sent twenty-four members of the European Parliament (MEPs) to the headquarters of the European Parliament in Brussels, more than any other UK political party. It was as strong a message as there ever has been that Britain is discontented with our continuing membership of the European Union.

The EU is a staggeringly expensive club. It costs us £55 million every day to stay in, yet it wastes billions on staffing costs, huge glitzy buildings, vanity projects, foreign junkets for MEPs, advertising, and moving the whole of the parliament to Strasbourg once a month, among other profligacies such as the 140 'embassies' it has set up in non-EU countries (forty-four diplomats in Barbados alone). It forces laws, directives and regulations on us whether we like them or not. It negotiates our trade deals for us and piles red tape on businesses. It controls how our farmers and our fishermen work. It dictates our energy policy, forcing us to add 'green taxes' which hike up fuel bills. It tells us we must open our borders to the 450 million people living in the other twenty-seven member states. We are required to submit to the rulings of the European Court of

Justice and the European Court of Human Rights, which can fine our businesses for breaching EU regulations and prevent us deporting dangerous foreign criminals. In addition to our membership fees, it makes us stump up further billions to bail out other member countries' economic failures.

Britain does not need any of this. We would be better off out.

No wonder UKIP won the European elections. Voters wanted UKIP MEPs to be their eyes and ears in Brussels and expose the truth about the stitch-ups, the profligacy, the posturing and the fundamental anti-democratic machinations behind the institution that would have us become citizens of a United States of Europe. The writing is on the wall; the EU flag, rather than the Union flag is now on our car number plates, driving licences and flying outside public buildings. In due course, the plan is to stamp the EU flag across all tiers of public administration. This includes replacing the royal crest on birth certificates with the circle of golden stars – all because of the Lisbon Treaty which Blair and Brown approved without reference back to the UK parliament or the electorate.

This all makes the old political parties deeply uneasy. They cannot fathom the public unrest at this kind of behaviour and prefer to turn their ire on UKIP, rather than on the EU. Licking their wounds after their election defeat, they argued it was 'pointless' voting to send UKIP MEPs to Europe because they would not engage in the processes of parliament and did not really want to be there. Putting aside the disdain this shows for voters, what they really meant was 'we don't want UKIP here messing things up for us'. They are right to be worried – UKIP MEPs expose how the three old parties vote to expand the EU and its supranational takeover bid, usually in stark contrast to whatever their leaders may be saying back home.

In one sense though, they *are* right: Nigel Farage has likened the role of UKIP MEPs to that of 'turkeys who would vote for Christmas' because we do want to get out of the EU, not engage with it.

Our MEPs would like to see themselves out of a job before the next planned Euro election in five years' time. In a more fundamental way though, the old parties were also very wrong: it is in fact pointless sending any MEPs to Brussels, whatever their political party.

Brussels: it's no place for democracy

The European Parliament bears little relation to our own parliament which, whatever you think of it, is at least democratic. The elected government of the day drafts legislation which MPs vote on. We have access to our MPs, we can write to them, phone or visit them asking them to either vote one way or another on our behalf and we can appeal to them for help with any problems we may have personally. Depending on how well or otherwise they perform their duties to us and our country, we can either vote for them again, or vote them out at the next election.

The European Parliament is completely different. MEPs have no say whatsoever in generating new legislation or re-visiting existing legislation. That is the sole preserve of the twenty-eight members of the EU Commission, one for each of the current member states. These commissioners are not elected, but appointed, meaning they are unaccountable; no one voted them in and so no one can vote them out. They are glorified bureaucrats. Yet only they can initiate legislation, so they are the ones that have all the power. MEPs can debate what the commissioners propose in committee meetings, ask questions of them, and suggest amendments which are then put to the vote in the EU Parliament, but that is all.

UKIP believes this is wrong. The complete lack of transparency and democratic accountability in those who would make decisions affecting our lives, our livelihoods and our public services is one very good reason to leave the EU. We believe anyone who has power over us should be democratically elected, not appointed. We should be able to kick them out of power via the ballot box if we so choose.

Let's get our sovereignty back

The goal of the EU is ever-increasing political union. UKIP is opposed to this and wants to see full powers for governance of Britain returned to us from the EU and placed back in the hands of our MPs in Westminster, and the British public, through the use of binding referenda. We do not want to be ruled by an out-of-sight, out-of-touch European bureaucratic elite.

At the moment, the EU makes most of our laws, although precisely what percentage is a topic of fierce debate. In a visit to Britain in February 2014, Viviane Reding, the European Commissioner for Justice, Fundamental Rights and Citizenship, addressed a meeting in London and stated that 70 per cent of laws in Britain are 'co-decided' with the EU. She subsequently reiterated the point, saying:

> I do not know if it is now 80 per cent or if it is 75 per cent. The truth is that most laws which are applied and executed, implemented at national level are based on European directives, which then have to be translated into national laws. So the most, the biggest part of the legislation which is applied in a given member state, in one of the twenty-eight, is decided by the European Parliament in co-decision with the Council of European Ministers.

A 2010 House of Commons Library report stated: 'The British government estimate around 50 per cent of UK legislation with a significant economic impact originates from EU legislation.'[13] Yet, in his famous televised debate with Nigel Farage, Liberal Democrat leader Nick Clegg quoted the same report and claimed the figure was just 7 per cent. However, the report actually says: 'Over the twelve-year period from 1997 to 2009, 6.8 per cent of primary legislation *and* 14.1 per cent of secondary legislation had a role in implementing EU obligations', so Nick was wrong and the figures

---

13   'How much legislation comes from Europe?', House of Commons Library research
     paper 10/62, 13 October 2010.

were five years out of date anyway. The conclusion of the very same report probably had it right: 'There is no totally accurate, rational or useful way of calculating the percentage of national laws based on or influenced by the EU.'

In any case, because in any case this argy-bargy misses the point. The EU controls immigration, business and employment, financial services, fishing, farming, law and order, energy and trade. So, whatever the precise figure is regarding how much British legislature is controlled by the EU, you can be sure it is too much.

Our voting power within the EU is also getting weaker and weaker. Those who say if we left the EU we would be isolated and lose our influence are being ridiculous: we have very little influence anyway. Since 1996, the UK has voted 'no' to a proposal fifty-five times at the Council of Ministers – where national ministers from each EU country meet to actually decide the EU's line on major issues – yet every single time the measure has gone on to become British law anyway.[14] We are unlikely ever to be able to get a 'no' vote carried unless a majority of the rest of the Union agrees, since the UK's voting power has declined as the EU has expanded. Research by campaign group Business for Britain says that, since 1973 the UK's voting power in the Council of Ministers has decreased from 17 to 8 per cent, in the European Parliament it has decreased from 20 to 9.5 per cent and in the European Commission it has decreased from 15 to 4 per cent.

When the Lisbon Treaty took effect on 1 December 2009, Britain lost its right of veto in more than forty areas of public policy. These included asylum, border controls, common defence policy, crime prevention incentives, criminal law, culture, emergency international aid, the EU budget, freedom to establish a business, intellectual property, police cooperation, self-employment rights, space, sport, tourism, transport and, significantly, withdrawal of a member state.

---

14   Press release issued by Business for Britain with research based on Freedom of Information requests, 24 March 2014.

Yet this was the treaty on which David Cameron broke his 'cast-iron' promise to give us a referendum.

Who voted for a United States of Europe?

No one did. The British people have never really had a vote on whether or not we should join in political union with other European nations. We joined what was the European Economic Community (EEC) in 1973 when parliament decided we should (and when the French finally agreed to let us in). A referendum held in 1975 asked whether we should stay in and 67 per cent of the 25 million who voted said 'yes', perhaps sensibly, because they were lied to and told we were simply entering a trading union, a 'common market' as the EEC was deliberately, and misleadingly, nicknamed for the purpose. So we stayed in and that, to date, has been that. No one under the age of fifty-seven has ever had a chance to have a say on the matter of leaving the EU, and no one has been allowed to vote on successive treaties that relinquished more and more of our sovereign powers and led to ever-deeper political union. Despite numerous 'cast-iron' promises from both Labour and Conservative politicians, all talk of referenda on any of these treaties has come to naught.

Given the massive difference between the EU now and then, how many of those 17 million who voted 'yes' in 1975 would do the same today? When they ticked the box on their referendum ballot, did they foresee they would be sending MEPs to Brussels to pay homage to a European national anthem and join parades in which the EU flag was marched around the city? Did they vote to give our MPs in Westminster less and less power? No. What has actually transpired since is disgraceful – some would say treacherous – yet only UKIP is seriously challenging any of it.

None of the other three main party leaders want to leave the EU. They would be quite happy to continue selling us down the river on Europe. They would not even be talking about Europe except in adulatory terms were it not for the rise of UKIP. Ed Miliband has pledged his commitment to staying in and defies calls to back a fresh referendum on membership. Nick Clegg has described the Liberal Democrats as 'the party of in' and will not budge. David Cameron might now be declaring himself 'eurosceptic', and 'proving it' with public bravado against the appointment of arch-federalist Jean-Claude Juncker as President of the EU Commission, but he has stated publicly that he wants to see the EU enlarged 'from the Atlantic to the Urals'[15] and he is supportive of Albania's application to join the EU. His MEPs too have consistently voted to allow new member states to join. In July 2014, shortly after their election, new Conservative MEPs in the European Parliament chose to demonstrate just how 'eurosceptic' they really are and how much they defend and recognise democracy by voting *against* allowing the Lithuanian people to hold a referendum on whether or not to join the Euro.

The EU: astronomically expensive, wasteful and riddled with fraud

An explanation of how much the EU costs us could get long, complicated and rather boring. Shall we keep it very simple and a tad more interesting?

At its most basic, we pay the EU a lot more than we get back. Not once in the last thirty-eight years have we got out more than we have put in (interestingly, the only year we ran a small surplus with the EU was 1975, the year of our referendum). Britain is the EU's second largest net contributor to EU funds after Germany. Currently, our gross contribution works out at around £55 million per day, or £20.5 billion annually. However, that does not include the UK rebate (the money we get back each year) nor our receipts from the EU budget. Please do

---

15   Speech made to students in the former Soviet republic of Kazakhstan, 1 July 2013.

not let this impress you too much – this money is, after all, only UK taxpayers' cash being given back to us via the Brussels middle-man.

In total between 1979 and 2012, Britain paid in about €260 billion to the EU. In that time we received just €163 billion back. The difference of €97 billion has been Britain's subsidy to the European project so far.[16]

We would be paying less, or more accurately getting more back, if, in 2007, Tony Blair had not given up 20 per cent of the rebate former Prime Minister Margaret Thatcher negotiated in 1984. Since much poorer countries have joined the EU there have been calls to scrap the rebate altogether. The UK has so far resisted this and, at present, still has a right of veto. But for how long? The pressure will increase if, as planned, the EU admits membership to countries already accepted as official candidates – Albania, Iceland, Macedonia, Montenegro, Serbia and Turkey – and potential candidates Bosnia Herzegovina and Kosovo. The former Soviet states of Moldova, Ukraine and Georgia have also expressed interest in joining.

Our financial contributions to the EU will only rise as poorer countries join. Certainly our payments show no sign of falling. Interestingly, we are paying more to the EU under the current Conservative-led government than we were under the more obviously pro-European Labour government. In the last three years of the Labour government under Gordon Brown, our net contributions totalled £11.7 billion. In the first three years of the coalition we paid over £25 billion net.

Of course the monetary cost of EU membership is more than just the net figure on the balance sheet of direct fiscal costs and benefits. There are additional costs of implementing EU legislation such as waste, fraud, lost jobs, and the higher food, fuel and water costs we pay as a result of our membership to consider. Any measurement of costs also has to take unemployment into account. Since the UK labour market is open to migrant labour from the rest of the EU, and

16   'How much does Britain pay into the EU and what does it get back?', www.thisismoney. co.uk, 1 August 2012.

because employment processes are reduced by unnecessary restrictions and regulations, British workers are finding it more difficult to get jobs and small businesses are going under. Taking economist Professor Tim Congdon's estimates of the total costs of membership at 11 per cent of gross domestic product (GDP), or what we produce as a nation, which comes to roughly £165–70 billion, then membership of the EU costs each British household a staggering £6,000 per year.[17] However, this figure does not include the additional £12.5 billion in bailouts Britain has paid to prop up the eurozone when countries such as Greece, Ireland and Portugal faced bankruptcy. That, according the *Daily Mail*, has cost every family in Britain another £500.[18]

UKIP recognises that Britain cannot afford to go on subsidising this undemocratic, bureaucratic and ultimately failing European project. It is time to quit and put the money we will save into supporting our own people, our own businesses and our own economy here at home.

The sleazy side of Europe

Especially galling, given the billions we send to the EU, is the fact that so much of our money is spent irresponsibly or lost to fraud and corruption.

The EU seems incapable of controlling its spending. In 2012, it paid out nearly £6 billion in 'error,' 23 per cent up on the 'errors' of 2011. Britain had to pick up an £800 million share of the extra bill.

Officially – yes, officially – the EU admits fraudulent activity costs the EU budget over €400 million annually. However in 2013, the House of Lords' European Union Select Committee published the results of an investigation into the matter which concluded the

---

17 *How Much Does the EU Cost Britain?* by Professor Tim Condon, published by the UK Independence Party, 2013.
18 12 February 2012.

true cost was far worse, up to twelve times as bad, and that the EU had 'failed to grasp the scale of the problem'. They said the price of EU fraud was more likely to be around €5 billion (£4.3 billion) every year, or 'maybe even more'. Bribery, corruption, cigarette smuggling, agriculture subsidies and payments for projects in the poorest countries that did not actually exist were among the reasons given for the massive losses.

Supporting the world's most expensive bureaucrats

Around 35 per cent of the EU's €1,756 billion annual budget goes on staffing costs. Faceless EU bureaucrats are among the best paid anywhere in the world. The President of the EU Commission (currently the infamous Jean-Claude Juncker) gets a salary of nearly €307,000 and an ordinary commissioner receives nearly €250,000 a year. Both get an additional 15 per cent of their salary to cover accommodation expenses, plus entertainment allowances, generous transitional payments when they leave office, plus a lifetime pension.

It is said that between them, Neil and Glenys Kinnock received more than £10 million in pay, allowances and pension entitlements during their time working at the European Union in Brussels. This included: £775,000 in wages for Lady Kinnock and £1.85 million for her husband, adding up to £2,625,000; allowances for Lady Kinnock's staff and office costs of £2.9 million; a £64,564 'entertainment allowance' for Lord Kinnock; five publicly funded pensions worth £4.4 million (allowing them to retire on £183,000 a year); and a housing allowance that allowed them both to claim accommodation costs although, as a married couple, they lived in the same house in the Belgian capital between 1995 and 2004.[19] Neither was elected, remember. Nice work if you can get it.

---

19   'Revealed: How the Kinnocks have enjoyed an astonishing £10 million ride on the EU gravy train', *Daily Mail*, 14 June 2009.

Where your money goes: spas, limos and golf courses

Even more scandalous is the money frittered away on ridiculous or unnecessary and unjustifiable expenditure. The TaxPayers' Alliance and Open Europe are both prime hunting grounds for anyone wishing to explore this in more detail, and among the extravagances they have highlighted are:

- €8.5 billion on a failed project to improve infrastructure in Sicily
- €2.4 billion annually on advertising the EU – a larger advertising budget than Coca-Cola's
- £150 million each year moving the EU Parliament in Brussels to Strasbourg once a month
- €5.25 million for a fleet of limousines for MEPs in Strasbourg
- €5.1 million to create a 'culture club' for EU bureaucrats in Luxembourg
- €1.6 million to the Swedish king to cover financial losses
- €900,000 for a golf course, hotel and spa whose guests included German Chancellor Angela Merkel
- €411,000 on a Hungarian fitness centre for dogs – which it is believed has never been built
- €40,000 on luxury gifts, including Tiffany jewellery
- €16,000 to Tyrolean farmers to boost their 'emotional connection with the landscape'

Is it any wonder auditors have refused to sign off the EU's accounts for the last nineteen years?

Referendum tomfoolery

Are you worried that if you vote UKIP you will not get a referendum? Don't be. Cameron has spun a nice line by offering an in/out referendum if he is the Prime Minister in a majority government after the 2015 general election, but it is meaningless. As UKIP's migration spokesman, Steven Woolfe, says: 'UKIP voters can see through this; they gave up on Cameron's lip service a long time ago and know who they can trust. They can pick apart all the spin to reveal what lies beneath: a failing party in desperate self-preservation mode.'

Cameron is a committed Europhile. He promises to renegotiate the terms of our EU membership, but has not started the process, will not give any clear indication of what terms he wishes to renegotiate or what criteria will be used to measure success. Cameron's pledge is tokenistic hot air with only one purpose: to crush the UKIP vote and sweep him to power. It is business as usual for a PM who is all spin and no substance.

Cameron will not be able to renegotiate on any matter of importance. Any change to the conditions of British membership would require the backing of the other twenty-seven member states, and how likely is that to happen? Are poor countries such as Slovakia, Romania, Bulgaria and Slovenia going to vote to give Britain, one of the wealthiest countries in Europe, any special privileges? Even if by some miracle they do – and if by a second miracle they find the time to push all this through – what one country wants, another will then want too. Any major renegotiation of terms by any one EU member state is likely to lead to the complete unravelling of the sacred European project so beloved by other members. The powers-that-be see the writing on the wall and will simply not allow any significant renegotiation to happen. Cameron knows this full well but does not really care. All he and the Conservatives need to do is peddle all the right lines to try and win over UKIP voters and pull the wool over the eyes of the rest. Cameron's referendum pledge is really about maintaining power at any price.

In any case, both Cameron and Juncker have confirmed that the free movement of people within EU member states is not up for renegotiation, not on any terms. So, one of the most pressing issues of our time, and the reason most people want to leave the EU, cannot and will not be changed.

Our Prime Minister had to fight tooth and nail to get the simple right to vote on the appointment of the new EU Commission President, and he lost twenty-six votes to two – despite the fact that most of the other voters didn't much like Juncker either. A deal was done, and we were on the wrong side of it. Note to Europhiles: Cameron's humiliation highlights once again just how impotent we have become in terms of influence.

During the Juncker debacle, the German *Der Spiegel* magazine reported how Cameron had threatened to call an immediate referendum if the former Luxembourg Prime Minister and arch-federalist was appointed to the EU's top job. During the horse-trading that took place, Cameron apparently told German Chancellor Angela Merkel he couldn't guarantee the UK staying in the EU if that happened. How about carrying out that threat, Dave?

Perhaps we have called his bluff. Cameron is not famous for keeping his word after all.

Voting Conservative will not deliver a referendum. Even if Cameron does manage to form a majority government – which is highly unlikely according to the polls – given his pro-EU stance, any referendum and any renegotiations are likely to be fudged.

Back in 1974 and 1975, ahead of the last EU referendum, Harold Wilson also made a commitment to renegotiation. He admitted that while he had not got everything he wanted, he had won 'big and significant improvements' (in practice, little more than a change to the tariff on New Zealand butter that had already been agreed). He then asked for votes in favour of continued membership, ensuring that the 'Yes' campaign outspent the 'No' campaign ten times over. His government issued a booklet that was sent to every household in Britain, written in language that was anything but neutral. While several pages were devoted to the 'benefits' of EU membership, only one page explored the negatives. Quite some trick, given where we

are now. What are the chances of Cameron doing the same? Nigel
Farage claims to already have evidence that the political class, cov-
ertly backed by its EU counterparts, are already trying to mislead
us again.[20]

The next time you hear Cameron speak the word 'referendum,'
substitute it for another three 'r' words to truly understand his meaning: rhetoric, rhetoric, rhetoric.

If you want a genuine referendum on UK membership of the EU,
the only way to get one is to back UKIP in the general election and
prevent either Conservative or Labour winning a majority. If UKIP
holds the balance of power, we can force an immediate referendum
so Britain can decide whether to stay in the EU or come out and claw
back independent power over our national life.

Better off out

Only when we have left the EU can we start to fix the massive problems we have in Britain and put the money the EU wastes to good
use here at home.

Out of the EU we can we regain control of our borders and control immigration. We can trade, but not be in political union, with
our European neighbours, and trade we would – we are the EU's
largest export market and they depend on us for jobs, not the other
way around. We can stop 'health tourism' which costs the NHS anything between £30 million and £2 billion a year, depending on whose
figures you believe. We can prevent foreign criminals entering the
country and deport those who commit crimes when here. We can
make sure British workers have first call on British jobs. Expensive
EU white elephants such as the HS2 rail link can be scrapped, as can
bill-hiking green taxes and wind turbine subsidies. We can replace the
Common Agricultural Policy and Common Fisheries Policy – which

cost us £10.3 billion and £2.81 billion respectively – with fairer payments and more effective conservation measures.

Given the EU's innumerable dictats, controls, blunders and its reckless and frequently unaccountable spending, there is only one common-sense vote at the ballot box, and that is a vote for UKIP, a vote that says we are better off out.

Vote UKIP to:

- Leave the EU and make our own laws
- Trade with the world, on our own terms
- Put an extra £170 billion a year to good use here at home
- End open-door immigration and control our borders
- Deport foreign criminals
- Reduce pressure on public services such as schools, housing and the NHS
- Give British residents priority for jobs
- Cut fuel bills by removing EU green taxes
- Give farmers and fishermen a better deal

Chapter 2

Common-Sense Immigration

A vote for UKIP is a vote for the fairest, most ethical and least racist immigration policy being put forward by any British political party; it is a vote to welcome into our country migrants with the skills needed to grow our economy and enhance vital public services, while taking back control of our borders and easing the immense pressure on schools, housing, welfare and the NHS.

For UKIP, immigration has never been about race, but space. The Office for National Statistics (ONS) reports that the number of people living on our tiny island has soared to over sixty-four million for the first time, with 39 per cent of the increase attributable to the fact that there more immigrants arriving in the country than there are people emigrating abroad.[21] Nearly 680 of us are already packed into each square mile and within the next twenty-five years it is estimated the UK will be home to *at least* ten million more people. Our population has grown twice as fast as the rest of Europe in the last decade alone.

Talking about this is not good enough. Politicians have to act. Poll after poll shows immigration is now the number one concern for the British people, and so it should be. After years of playing the issue down – and often trying to shut it down with allegations of racism – the people's concerns are all too clearly borne out by the

---

21   All figures in this chapter are based on information from the Office for National Statistics unless otherwise stated.

figures and the dramatic social and economic impact their reckless-
ness has had on Britain.

Mass immigration has coincided with soaring youth unemployment and stagnant wages that have not kept pace with the cost of
living. While nearly one million British young people cannot find
jobs, one million more migrants from Eastern Europe have found
minimum wage jobs here in the last decade. The welfare bill soars.
Public services are under severe pressure: parents struggle to find
school places for their children; getting a GP or hospital appointment or finding an NHS dentist gets ever more difficult; transport
systems are straining at the seams. There is huge demand on fuel,
so we become increasingly reliant on dictatorships with appalling
human rights records. Demand for housing has never been higher;
we need to build a new house every seven seconds to keep up with
demand from our growing population, a crazy state of affairs that
puts our countryside and precious green space at risk. How long
before Britain is completely concreted over at this rate and ours is
no longer a green and pleasant land?

To put it very bluntly, we simply can't go on like this. Uncontrolled
immigration has to stop. And only UKIP has fair, workable, non-
racist immigration policies to solve the problem of overcrowded
Britain.

You can't trust other parties on immigration

UKIP's approach is in stark contrast to the shocking way in which the
old parties handle immigration. It is nigh on impossible to believe
it now, but the Labour Party came to power in 1997 on a manifesto
promise to take 'firm control over immigration'. What a joke. Tony
Blair opened Britain up to the world and Gordon Brown continued
in his footsteps. The annual net migration figure quadrupled under
Labour, from 48,000 people in 1997 to 198,000 by 2009.

Now, Labour leader Ed Miliband is quite happy to admit that

'Labour got it wrong on immigration' as is former Labour Home Secretary Jack Straw, who, with astonishing hypocrisy, has said it was a 'spectacular mistake' to let so many people settle here.

A 'mistake'? No. Ed, Jack, you know you are both wrong: there was no 'mistake'. Your Labour government deliberately, and with bewildering disregard for the consequences, encouraged massive immigration.

According to Andrew Neather, former speechwriter for Jack Straw and Tony Blair, the two of them conspired to promote immigration to utterly transform the social, cultural and demographic make-up of Britain simply to 'rub the right's nose in diversity'. Neather was the author of a landmark speech in September 2000 by the then immigration minister, Barbara Roche, which called for a loosening of immigration controls. Labour sent out search parties around the globe to entice immigrants to Britain, Peter Mandelson has admitted. Mandelson, a former EU Trade Commissioner, has also conceded that the influx of new arrivals is why traditional supporters of the Labour Party are now unable to find work.

Needless to say, at the time all this was deliberately concealed from the public. It was possibly one of the most treacherous periods in British history when it comes to government concealment.

Labour must never again be trusted with power, their record on the economy and immigration is simply too horrifying.

Labour: shutting down debate with just one word

Not only did Labour engineer a dramatic influx of migrants to denigrate traditional Britishness and enforce extreme left-wing ideology, they also shut down debate on immigration by ruthlessly accusing anyone who dared question them of racism, possibly the worst kind of 20th- and 21st-century thought-crime you could be guilty of.

It is often the small events in history that resonate the loudest and prove to be a catalyst for change. When Rochdale pensioner and life-long Labour voter Gillian Duffy challenged Gordon Brown while he was on a walkabout in the area, asking him 'What are you going to do about immigration?' he called her a 'bigot' and, finally, politicians – and the media – woke up.

No one with genuine concerns about the scale of immigration should be labelled a bigot or racist. At least the Gillian Duffy incident was a turning point, of sorts. It was certainly a green light for politicians in both the red and the blue corner to crank up the rhetoric of immigration once again.

The Conservatives took over government in 2010 promising to cut net migration to the 'tens of thousands'. They have failed abysmally. In 2013, net migration increased by some 60,000 on 2012, rocketing up to 212,000.

This all adds up to a massive administration bill even before we start to talk about illegal immigration.

It was recently revealed that sixteen allegedly illegal immigrants have fought deportation for a combined forty-two years, at a cost of £100 each per day. The total bill so far for their bed and board is £1.5 million.[22] Altogether, holding suspected illegal immigrants in detention centres costs £100 million a year and another £50 million goes on actual deportations.

When it comes to EU migration however, there can be no deportations, no matter how high the numbers rise. As long as we remain in the EU and are forced to obey EU laws we must keep our borders open to all-comers.

Over half of last year's net migration figure – 141,000 people – is the result of migrants from within the EU. Of these, 65,000 were from so-called EU15 countries, mostly poor, former communist countries who only became members in 2004, almost a three-fold increase on the previous year. Between 2004 and 2011 the number of Poles living in the UK leapt from 69,000 to 687,000 (Poles are now the second largest immigrant group in the UK after Asian Indians, and Polish is the UK's second most widely spoken language). Approximately 24,000 citizens of Romania and Bulgaria arrived in 2013, also nearly three times the number of the previous year – a 166 per cent increase. Even Labour's former Home Secretary David Blunkett – another immigration co-conspirator – is now complaining about Roma gypsies in his home town of Sheffield, saying they are causing 'understandable tensions' with their littering and refusal to send their children to school.[23] Interestingly, he was accused of 'feeding Romaphobia' by *The Guardian*.[24] There is some justice in this world.

David Cameron cannot help Blunkett. He knows he is unable to 'renegotiate' the issue of free movement across borders. The President of the EU Commission, Jean-Claude Juncker, has made this abundantly clear to him. In any case, Cameron has not committed to trying to renegotiate this – he has not actually committed to trying to renegotiate anything ahead of his make-believe referendum.

Tory and Labour fail: time for UKIP

Labour promises to cut immigration and then does the opposite. The Conservatives promise to cut immigration but they simply cannot, as UKIP has always predicted. While we remain in the European Union, and while the EU insists on the free movement of citizens of member states across borders, immigration will never be controlled, so it is pointless for governments to set targets.

Set targets they do though, and to meet them, they can only limit non-EU migration. Because an unskilled, non-English-speaking labourer from the EU has an absolute right to live, work

---

23   Interview with BBC Radio Sheffield, November 2013.

24   'David Blunkett is feeding "Romaphobia"' by Jake Bowers, *The Guardian*, 13 November 2013.

and settle in the UK, we must close the doors on qualified scientists, doctors or engineers from Australia or Canada if we are to cut net migration. Citizens from former English-speaking Commonwealth countries are treated with a second-class status when it comes to migrating to Britain.

So what would UKIP do? First, let us be crystal clear: UKIP's policy is to support *controlled* immigration, not stop it altogether. We need immigration and we recognise it can enrich our country if handled properly. It is shameful how, because it has been allowed to spiral out of control and cause problems, 'immigration' has become almost a dirty word. UKIP wants to give immigration its positive image back, and we will do this not by 'pulling up the drawbridge' but by doing what every other sensible nation on earth does: controlling who walks over the drawbridge, and deciding who that should be in a way that is fair and equitable.

UKIP would not forcibly repatriate anyone, apart from foreign criminals. UKIP simply advocates a sensible, points-based immigration system that restores our faith in the value of migrants and makes sure those who come to Britain contribute to Britain and uphold British values and law.

UKIP believes in applying this same points-based immigration system to *everyone* who wants to come and live in Britain, irrespective of where they come from in the world and regardless of their race, their religion or their colour. Unlike the current system, which is unfair, unworkable and arguably racist in that it allows free entry to anyone from the predominantly white, Christian EU, while vetting and vetoing mostly black and Asian citizens from the former Commonwealth, UKIP's immigration policy is truly egalitarian.

UKIP will end open-door immigration and welcome into Britain those who are able to show they can support themselves (and their families where applicable) without access to welfare or services such as state education or social housing for at least five years. This move alone will radically cut the numbers of new migrants choosing to come to Britain and swiftly reduce the welfare bill. In tandem with this, a UKIP government would withhold all state benefits from migrants for a period of five years, over which time they would have to be paying into the system through tax and national insurance to claim.

We would insist new migrants have private healthcare insurance as only emergency treatment would be offered freely on the NHS. Proof of private health insurance would also be a condition for tourists entering the UK.

Time-limited work permits would only be given to those who have skills we need. In order to give our unemployed a chance and halt downward pressure on already low wages, we would prevent minimum wage jobs being offered directly to overseas workers. Obviously those already living here could apply as usual.

UKIP would also take a firm approach to border control and increase UK Border Agency staff as appropriate. There would be no amnesty for illegal immigrants or failed asylum seekers and we would also make speaking competent English a condition of entry.

We would continue to take our fair share of refugees and asylum seekers, in line with our record on this: it was UKIP who first protested against the coalition's initial refusal to take in refugees fleeing the Syrian civil war. Those escaping from appalling situations in their home countries, and who fulfil United Nations criteria, need safe havens, and Britain will remain one of them. However, out of the EU, we will not be obliged to take refugees who obtain an EU passport, as we are at the moment.

These are tough measures, but they are needed in tough times. Britain is at breaking point and immigration must be tackled. The people of Britain expect hard-hitting action after the suffering many have experienced as a result of Labour's abysmal policies and the Conservatives' continuing flirtation with the EU which leaves them impotent on immigration. They also deserve nothing less. UKIP is the only party that can be trusted to get the job done.

Vote UKIP to:

- Control our own borders outside the EU
- End open-door immigration
- Apply the same points-based immigration system to everyone, equally
- Insist migrants must support themselves for a minimum of five years
- Stop state benefits for new migrants unless they have paid tax and NI for five years
- No immigration for minimum wage jobs
- Deport illegal immigrants and failed asylum seekers
- Welcome genuine asylum cases

Chapter 3

Trading with the World and Protecting Jobs

A vote for UKIP is a vote to trade with the world on our terms; retake our seat on the World Trade Organization; re-establish trade links with the Commonwealth, remove business from massive EU overregulation; give British job seekers priority and stop advertising 800,000 UK-based vacancies to EU workers.

'Isolationists.' 'Little Englanders.' When it comes to a debate on world trade and UKIP, these two slurs from our detractors probably come out top, yet even a cursory examination of the facts reveals the hidden truth: it is precisely because of our continued EU membership that Britain is becoming ever more isolated in the world, ever more like 'little Englanders', and less and less like Great Britons.

When Europhiles use the word 'isolationist', what they imply is that they do not want a Britain which is independent, democratic and self-governing. They eschew this positive vision for Britain's future in favour of it becoming 'an offshore province in a country called Europe' as Roger Helmer MEP so succinctly put it.[25]

Helmer writes:

---

25   Roger Helmer MEP writing for *UKIP Daily*: '*The Economist* gets it wrong. Again.', 19 November 2013.

UKIP has a much bigger and brighter vision for Britain's future: one as a major global player in which we move out of the EU, and into the world. This means having a free trade deal with our European neighbours. It means resuming our seat in the World Trade Organization. It means being part of innumerable international organisations including the UN Security Council, NATO, the Commonwealth, the World Bank and dozens more. It means resuming our natural role as a global trading nation. It's a strange use for the word 'isolation'.

EU trade myths

Britain is currently the world's sixth largest economy and the third largest economy in Europe, after Germany and France. The fourth largest exporter of goods worldwide, the UK is also the world's top international financial centre. We are in a strong position when it comes to global trade and do significantly better than most other EU countries. However, the importance of Europe and the eurozone in global commerce has been in general decline over the past twenty-five years (with peaks and troughs). In 1980, the EU's share of global wealth (world GDP) was over 30 per cent. Now, it is less than 20 per cent and is projected to fall to 15 per cent by 2050.[26]

With the emergence of rapidly developing new markets in Asia and South America, the EU's percentage of global trade suggests little indication of recovering any time soon. As a world player, the EU zone is shrinking and we will inevitably shrink with it if we stay in. At the moment, less than 5 per cent of UK businesses trade with Europe, only 10 per cent of our economy is accounted for by exports to EU countries, and less than half our exports are destined for the EU, yet 100 per cent of our businesses are subject to the sum total of all EU regulations. We are stuck in a ridiculous vicious circle: while we export less and less each year (and estimates from Global Britain, a

---

think tank which analyses trade figures, suggest the EU may account for only 20 per cent of UK exports by 2030), our annual gross contribution to EU institutions keeps on rising nevertheless.

Who in their right mind would want to shackle Britain to an economic area in long-term decline *and* pay over the odds for the privilege? Those who advocate doing so must either buy into the greater European project of ever-deepening political union – a position which renders their economic arguments at best superfluous and at worst irrelevant – or be so risk-averse they prefer to stick with the devil they know.

Britain: impotent and isolated on trade

Prior to joining the EU, Britain struck its own trade deals and traded freely with the rest of the world. We surrendered our trade negotiating rights when we signed up to what was then the EEC. Britain has not negotiated a single trade deal since 1975 and while we remain in the EU it will never negotiate one ever again.

'The EU treaties are crystal clear: only the European Commission may conduct trade for member states,' writes William Dartmouth MEP in his detailed analysis of the truths and falsehoods of Britain's trading position both in and outside the EU.[27] UKIP does not believe this is in Britain's best interests, advocating open and free trade and maintaining that the future success of UK trade policy lies in reactivating our seat at the WTO, where we have a voice and can negotiate as a full and independent member.

'Officially, all EU member states, including the UK, became members of the World Trade Organization [in 1995 and] retain seats at the WTO, but only, and this is crucial, as "observers",' Dartmouth explains. 'The effect is that the UK's seat on the WTO is purely symbolic, devoid of real power and meaning.'

---

27   *Out of the EU and Into the World* by William Dartmouth MEP, published by the then EFD group of the European Parliament.

The fact Britain has to get up and leave the table when the WTO holds global talks reveals just how stymied we have become on trade: while the tiny Isle of Man and the former British colony of Hong Kong have full negotiating competence within the WTO, Britain is not even a country on the world map as far as it is concerned – Brussels has seen to that. If you move your cursor over the WTO's interactive membership map on their website, you will even see there is no UK, France, Germany, Spain or any other EU member country listed because we are all lumped together as a country called 'European Union (formerly EC)'.

Out of the EU, as full members of the WTO, we would not be forced to leave our trade deals to a faceless, unelected bureaucrat who is obliged to put the needs of twenty-seven other countries on a level par with, or perhaps even above, UK interests. It is time to move outside the political structures of the EU and retain trading and economic links with member states through Swiss-style free trade agreements (FTAs). Switzerland has persistently refused to join the EU because Swiss citizens recognise that their high standard of living and quality of life would be severely compromised by doing so, yet the country enjoys a 67 per cent share of world GDP covered by FTAs. The EU zone meanwhile, takes just 30 per cent.[28]

The European Free Trade Association (EFTA), of which Switzerland is a member along with Norway, Iceland and Liechtenstein, also consistently runs a trade surplus with the EU, €22.3 billion in 2012. By contrast, the UK's trade deficit with the EU now runs at around £30 billion per year.[29] 'EFTA has also had its accounts signed off every year,' remarks Dartmouth. 'By comparison, the EU has not had its accounts signed off for nineteen years.'

---

28   Source: United Nations.
29   Report on 'The Annual Report on the functioning of the EEA Agreement in 2009', p.6, European Economic Area Joint Parliamentary Committee, Ref 1097634, 29 March 2010.

What of the argument that we gain 'insider advantage' by remaining EU members? The evidence does not stack up. A recent investigation by social policy think tank Civitas[30] showed that while there were twenty-five EU FTAs in force in 2012, the Swiss had independently negotiated twenty-six, thirteen of which came into force before those of the EU, and three in the same year. The report added that there was no evidence to suggest the quality of the EU's trade agreements were any higher nor that the 'heft' or 'clout' of the EU had helped secure more FTAs than those that might have been secured by independent negotiations anyway.

The report by corporate researcher Michael Burrage concluded: 'The evidence presented contradicts again and again those who wish to claim that the UK has enjoyed insider advantages in the single market.'

The government goes to great lengths to hide the reality of our impotence on trade from the British people, even sending ministers on far-flung 'trade missions' such as the one David Cameron himself led to China in December 2013. These so-called Prime Ministerial trade delegations are actually nothing more than grandiose attempts to make us all feel better about ourselves. The next time you hear of one remember this: Britain is not permitted to enter into any kind of trade directly with China, or with any other nation. Only the EU Trade Commissioner is allowed to negotiate trade agreements on behalf of *all* member states, and they will rightly – as that is their job – bear in mind the needs of *all* member states at the negotiating table, possibly compromising Britain's position and interests. Then, when it comes to approving trade agreements by vote at the Council of Ministers, remember our influence is now tiny – just 8 per cent and ever-declining as new member states join. Trade delegations have no teeth, no negotiating power, and no substance beyond being elaborate – and expensive – PR stunts with perhaps a little diplomacy thrown in on the side.

---

30   Civitas report, *Where's the Insider Advantage?* by Michael Burrage, 2014.

Trade, not political union

We do not need to be members of the European Union to trade with it. Twenty-nine countries outside the EU currently have trade deals in place with the EU and do big business. In 2012 China sold €290 billion worth of goods to EU member states; Russia €213 billion; the USA €205 billion. Switzerland and Norway, both geographically within Europe but part of the EFTA rather than the EU, conducted trade worth over €100 billion.[31]

'This is the huge "inconvenient truth" for the entire British political establishment,' says Dartmouth. 'Political union has nothing to do with and is irrelevant to trade – except, possibly, to inhibit it.'[32]

Or, as economist Tim Condon CBE puts it:

> We have not had to become the fifty-first state of the United States of America in order to sell almost £40 billion a year to it – more than we sell to France or Germany, our largest trading partners in the EU ... The EU is a big market for dozens of countries that do not belong to it; it would be a big market for the UK if we too did not belong to it.

It is within this context that we must view comments by politicians such as Deputy Prime Minister Nick Clegg when they tell us leaving the EU would be 'economic suicide'. It is a nice line in political scaremongering, but has no basis in fact.

The ante is sometimes upped when Europhiles suggest the EU would refuse to negotiate a trade deal with Britain if we left the Union, but why would they do that? Britain is the eurozone's biggest export market worldwide, the eurozone's biggest supplier worldwide, and the country with which the eurozone has the biggest trade surplus worldwide.[33] Is the EU seriously going to cut off its nose to spite its face if

---

31 Figures from Eurostat, the European Commission statistics database, and the World Bank.
32 *Out of the EU and Into the World* by William Dartmouth MEP, published by the former EFD group of the European Parliament.
33 Data from the May 2013 edition of the *Monthly Bulletin* of the European Central Bank, Table 7.2, 'Current and Capital Accounts', p.63.

Britain leaves? Will major German companies such as Mercedes, for example, for whom Britain is a profitable market, allow that to happen?

Speaking at the UKIP Conference in 2013, the former director general of the Confederation of British Industry (CBI), Lord Digby Jones, rejected this as a possibility, saying that leaving the EU would not be the 'unattractive option' that pro-Europeans claim, as the UK would be able to negotiate FTAs with the rest of the bloc 'the day after our exit'. He also slated David Cameron's promise of renegotiation and reform, saying he would only get minor adjustments here and there but not the sort of reform upon which our future membership should be conditional. 'If anyone, the CBI included, thinks that fundamental reform is on the EU agenda, they are deluding themselves,' he said. 'We certainly must put the option of leaving on the negotiating table ... the tactic of promising to stay in the EU regardless of what the Prime Minister can negotiate is insane.'

Building trade with the Commonwealth

Queen Elizabeth II is Head of the Commonwealth, the fifty-three countries that were mostly territories of the former British Empire. The Commonwealth is home to 2.2 billion people who, in many cases, share our language and our laws and, with whom, through history, we have a common bond. It is also a growing economy: while the EU's share of world GDP is currently around just 20 per cent and predicted to fall, the countries of the Commonwealth are growing fast, with growth of 7.2 per cent predicted for 2012–17.[34] Yet we have no direct trade links to the Commonwealth.

When we surrendered our powers to negotiate our own trade deals to the EU Trade Commissioner in 1975, we also had to abandon our longstanding trade relationships with Commonwealth countries, what were called the Ottowa Agreements, which had played such a

---

34   Commonwealth Growth Tracker, World Economics Report, 2013.

significant role in rescuing Britain from the Great Depression of the '30s. William Dartmouth MEP says of our severed links with the Commonwealth: 'The politicians of the '60s and '70s made the wrong choice.'

Over the last six years alone, the UK has run up a £105 billion trade deficit with the EU, while enjoying a £21 billion trade surplus with the rest of the world.[35] It is time to free ourselves from the shackles of the failing eurozone. As Roger Helmer MEP puts it: 'It's a choice between a dying Europe and a vibrant, growing world. It's a choice between staying buried in the bureaucratic nightmare of Brussels, or resuming our proper place in the rest of the world.'

Abolishing endless red tape

Outside of the EU, not only can we trade with the world, we can also free British businesses from the stranglehold of excessive regulation which costs us tens of billions of pounds a year,[36] undermines our industrial competitiveness and forces industries off-shore, industries which then take their jobs and their investment with them.

The Forum of Private Business conducted research into the cost of EU regulations and found costs rose by 4 per cent between 2012 and 2013 for businesses employing fewer than 250 people, equivalent to £700 per company and at a cost of £900 million overall. That was in just one year and despite relatively minor changes to the statute books.[37] Worse, the cost of compliance per employee was seven times higher for micro-employers, or very small businesses perhaps with a single business owner and less than twenty staff, than it was for medium-sized employers. Larger companies of course find it easier to absorb these costs – it is no coincidence that it is generally large companies represented by organisations such as the CBI who are the most likely to argue for remaining within the EU.

---

35   Source: the Office for National Statistics.
36   Open Europe suggest EU regulation costs the UK economy more than £27 billion annually.
37   The Forum of Private Business' July 2014 referendum 208 report.

The onslaught of regulations is neverending: some 4,000 additional regulations have been passed by the EU since 2010 and with each day more are devised and passed into legislature. It is almost as if EU commissioners sit in their offices wondering: 'How can we mess up someone's business today?'

The latest dictat is a requirement that British firms employing over 500 people will be required to publish an annual 'corporate social responsibility statement' detailing all manner of non-business related dogma such as their environmental impact, policies on diversity and human rights, how they are employing and promote staff of different ages, genders and 'educational and professional backgrounds', how they ensure 'respect for workers' rights' and facilitate talks with trade unions. Campaign group Better Off Out claims compliance with all this could add an extra £4,000 a year in administrative costs.[38]

Fewer than one in ten British businesses trade with the EU, yet 100 per cent of them still have to carry the burden of complying with thousands of EU laws on employment, waste management, environmental regulations, product registration, health and safety etc. China, the USA, Russia, Switzerland, Norway – all these non-EU countries which do business with the EU, conform to EU regulations when it comes to their exports but not their entire export industry or their whole economy, which is free from outside political interference. There are very strong arguments in favour of Britain doing the same, especially when it comes to supporting the millions of small businesses up and down the country which are the bedrock of the British economy. EU regulations do them the most harm.

Shropshire businessman Jonathan Carr has grown increasingly frustrated at how regulations have stacked the odds against staying in the business he has grown over the last twenty-five years and which now employs sixty-five people. A UKIP member, he maintains

---

38 'British firms fear red-tape hell as EU orders equality and green energy reports' by Macer Hall, *Daily Express*, 24 July 2014.

his business could be three to five times as big and employing several times more people than it does now but for the damaging effects of EU anti-business regulations:

> Firstly, we need to employ two people in non-productive roles simply to make sure we comply with numerous employment regulations, form filling and bureaucracy on top of all the taxes, licence fees etc. we pay. Just as damaging and costly, every year for the past fifteen years at least we have seen niche products that were a vital part of our business turnover, and which it had taken us years to develop into profitable lines, regulated out of existence. Every time that happens jobs and profitability are destroyed at manufacturer level and in our case distribution too. Even the couriers delivering to end customers lose business and jobs. In the vast majority of cases products go either because manufacturers cannot afford several hundreds of thousands of pounds to register a previously nationally approved product at EU level or the markets for the product are too small to justify that huge investment. This has been the case in the health food and vitamins business, herbal remedies, pesticides, animal health products and pharmaceuticals. Thousands of jobs have been destroyed in these and many other sectors of business by the EU.

It is hard not to be deeply cynical about just why big businesses lobby government so ferociously on the merits of EU membership when you hear Jonathan talk about outcomes in many such circumstances. 'Quite often I have seen products and their small UK manufacturers regulated out of business in this way only to find their product is then picked up by large companies (often European) who can afford the registration process and can afford to lobby and grease palms in Brussels,' he says. 'The product will then reappear a few years later, but at about three times the cost to the consumer and from a monopoly (European) supplier.'

Red tape favours big businesses that can afford the administrative staff to cope with the necessary registration requirements and numerous other employment, quality, environmental and other business standards requirements that act as an entrance barrier to smaller businesses in most trades. Regulation works in their favour – it reduces competition. Their cries that we will lose jobs and be poorer outside the EU are treated with scorn by Jonathan who says the very opposite is the case, and that without the dead hand of excessive regulation and EU bureaucracy, millions of small- and medium-sized businesses would be able to employ more people and there would be an explosion of growth in small to medium enterprises. He notes:

> The problem is too many people running businesses nowadays are too young to remember how simple it was before 1972 to set up and run a business. They therefore accept all the burdens imposed on them by the EU as the 'norm' and don't consider how much better off they would be without that burden. Like slaves, they are so used to being in chains they know no difference.

Saving British jobs

It is not difficult to find numerous examples of how the EU works actively against the best interests of British workers. In 2007 the Peugeot factory in Ryton, Coventry, closed down with 2,300 job losses and moved to Slovakia with the help of £78 million EU 'structural and cohesion' funding, plus £10 million from the UK government. Then in 2012, after forty years in production, the Ford Transit factory in Southampton closed down with the loss of 1,100 jobs and relocated to (non-EU) Turkey after receiving a £800 million loan from the European Investment Bank, the bank of the European Union. The loan was backed by Chancellor George Osborne. Effectively, the EU has used British taxpayers' money to put British workers on the dole.

There has been much controversy in Britain over post office

closures and the sell-off of the Royal Mail, both of which have brought job losses, yet what is less widely known because the old party politicians hide the issue, is that both of these are a direct consequence of the EU Postal Services Directive that was steered through the European Parliament by the Labour MEP Brian Simpson in 1997.[39] This directive put an end to the Royal Mail being able to cross-subsidise rural post offices and ended the important role as community hubs they had played for centuries.

These are three clear examples of how direct EU interference damages British jobs. Take the indirect ways in which we feel the impact and the examples appear to be endless.

Open borders and close the doors on British workers

The free movement of workers and job seekers across EU member state borders has severe implications for British people either in or looking for employment. When we joined the EU in 1973, all the other member countries had similar standards of living to us. Now, when many have a minimum wage of 80p an hour, we are experiencing wage compression at home and a 'skills drain' from those countries.

The EU's own data tells us that EU migrants are now more likely to be in work in Britain than Britons themselves.[40] 75.4 per cent of British citizens aged twenty to sixty-four were in work in 2013 compared with 79.2 per cent of EU nationals living here, suggesting migrants from Europe are taking jobs that might otherwise go to British applicants.

EURES, the EU-wide jobs portal, must shoulder some of the responsibility for this. It has become the 'go-to' source for employers

---

39   EU Directive, June 2008.
40   'EU migrants more likely to be in work than Britons' by David Barrett, *Daily Telegraph*, 30 July 2014.

looking for cheap labour from overseas and at any one time some 800,000 British jobs are advertised on the portal. When the *Daily Express* ran a story on this on 2 August 2014, the newspaper found that of the total 2.4 million jobs advertised, a third of them, 780,000, were based in Britain, compared to just two in Croatia.[41] UKIP's employment spokeswoman, Jane Collins MEP, told the *Express*:

> It is staggering that we are turning a blind eye to jobs that could be done by the majority of the 2.3 million unemployed in the UK which are being advertised in countries thousands of miles away. With unemployment rising across the eurozone it stands to reason this will lead to a flood of migrant workers, making it harder and harder for our own unemployed workforce to get a job.

Add to this the fact that unemployed non-British EU residents can get relocation grants of up to €1,000 to come and work in Britain, is it any wonder we have nearly one million unemployed young people in Britain who are finding it impossible to get a foot on the job ladder with even a minimum-wage job?

That said, even minimum-wage jobs are now subject to downward pressure. A report by the Migration Advisory Committee (MAC) published in July 2014 found rules on the National Minimum Wage are being routinely flouted and workers exploited. 'We came across some people who were working for £50 a week in food manufacturing,' the MAC Chairman was quoted as saying. 'A typical employer can expect a compliance visit just once every 250 years and a prosecution once in a million years. There is incomplete compliance with and enforcement of labour regulations, and regulatory resources and penalties are inadequate.'

The report concluded that: 'The impacts of migrants on average wages ... tended to be positive at the top of the wage distribution and

---

41 'Turning a blind eye to Brit workers: 780,000 UK jobs touted to Europeans' by Giles Sheldrick, *Daily Express*, 2 August 2014.

negative at the bottom.' The MAC committee also warned that any future expansion of the EU needed to be better managed, perhaps an understatement considering there are currently eight countries looking to join the EU, together containing ninety million people earning less than half of the average UK wage.

Some find it easy to say that we Brits are just too lazy or too greedy and need to work for the same wages that migrants do. Even putting aside the fact that paying below minimum wage is illegal, they miss the point: many of the migrants from poor countries in Eastern and Southern Europe have come from very little indeed and subsequently have little to lose by living in extremely cramped, dangerous conditions with several others, or indeed living on the streets. With average rents at £1500 a month, how else can they afford accommodation on minimum wages? Is this really the kind of unethical, unfulfilling working life we should condone for anyone in Britain?

The rise of zero-hour contracts

There has been much political hot air and countless column inches devoted to the explosion in use of zero-hour contracts which Ed Miliband has threatened to ban. Zero-hour contracts, where no fixed hours are set in advance, might suit some people who choose to work in this way, but it is generally accepted to be completely wrong to offer them as the only form of employment to employees seeking stable, regular work. Nigel Farage has said their use reminds him of the way dockers used to have to gather at the dock gates in the '20s and a foreman would come out and point to those he could use and tell the rest to go home with no money in their pockets. It is just not on to expect people to pay their bills and raise a family under employment conditions like this, and zero-hour contracts have rightly been widely questioned.

However, it is precisely because of EU regulations that they have proliferated. It is possible to track their increasing use directly from the introduction of the EU Temporary Agency Workers Directive which gave agency workers exactly the same rights in the workplace as employees. Clearly this was a devastating blow to many businesses on cost grounds alone, as the whole point of employing temporary workers is usually the flexibility they offer to provide maternity or sick cover, for example, without incurring the costs of taking on another employee. Open Europe claims the move is costing British businesses £2 billion annually but many companies, including large multi-nationals, simply by-pass the legislation through the use of zero-hour contracts. It is ironic that EU legislation intended to give rights to temporary workers and stop them being discriminated against in the workplace has in fact bred a plethora of zero-hour contracts which do precisely the opposite.

The 'three million jobs' myth

'The overall verdict is clear. EU membership has destroyed British jobs and done nothing to boost the productive efficiency and export competitiveness of our economy. From an employment perspective, EU membership has been strongly against our national interest,' wrote Tim Condon in his booklet *Europe Doesn't Work*.[42] So why does the pro-EU brigade frequently claim that leaving the EU will cost Britain three million jobs?

The 'three million jobs' myth is one of the most pernicious and ludicrous political lies ever told. A clear attempt to move the debate towards fear, it has no basis in fact.

The falsehood took hold following a report by the National Institute of Economic and Social Research (NIESR) in 2000. The report concluded that some 2.7 million jobs were directly related to trade with the EU and another 500,000 were indirectly linked, but it was

42   Published by the Hampden Trust in association with the Freedom Association 2013.

unlikely many of these jobs would be lost if Britain were to leave the EU. Jobs *linked* to EU trade is not at all the same thing as jobs *dependent* on EU trade, and it is trade that is the issue, not EU membership. When the figures were seized upon by Europhiles for propaganda purposes, and used to suggest three million jobs would be lost, the Director of NIESR, Martin Weale, repudiated that claim and described it as 'absurd … pure Goebbels. In many years of academic research I cannot recall such a wilful distortion of the facts.' [43]

Tim Farron, the Liberal Democrats' President, told a fringe event at his party conference in September 2013 that the three million jobs line should not be repeated as it was 'not credible'. Yet Nick Clegg doggedly repeated it several times during his debates with Nigel Farage ahead of the 2014 European elections. The word 'desperate' comes to mind.

Jobs across Europe depend on trade relationships, not EU membership. Businesses trade, not countries. In any case, more jobs in Europe depend on trade with the UK than vice versa, and the EU sells £28 billion more to us annually than we sell them.

The writer Frederick Forsyth hit the nail on the head when he said:

> The supposition is that the other twenty-seven nations of the EU, which jointly make a £163 billion a year trading surplus out of us, would simply launch a trade war and refuse to buy another pennyworth of British products. The fact that we could then do the reverse and cause the firing of five million European workers (which we would never do either) is never mentioned. [44]

Some jobs will almost certainly be lost, yes, but nothing like three million. The NIESR report stated only a fraction of that number would be in jeopardy if we left, and then only for a short time. What

---

43   An interview with *The Times*, 19 February 2000.
44   'The three million jobs myth: Euro fanatics such as Kenneth Clarke and Nick Clegg are still parroting this myth' by Frederick Forsyth, *Daily Express*, 18 July 2014.

we might lose on the swings, we would gain on the roundabout, as we forged our own worldwide trade deals, prioritised British workers for jobs and freed businesses from the straightjacket of excess regulation to encourage entrepreneurship and Britain's manufacturing industry.

The only jobs we would not be able to get back would be those of the seventy-three MEPs Britain sends to Brussels. For the ones who are members of UKIP, that day cannot come fast enough.

Vote UKIP to:

- Start trading with the EU and the world on our terms
- Reinstate our seat at the World Trade Organization
- Build trade links with emerging and growing, not declining economies
- Re-establish strong trade links with the Commonwealth
- Cut excessive and unnecessary regulations which hold business back
- Give British jobseekers priority for British jobs
- Stop advertising British jobs overseas, except where there is a well-defined need
- Regulate zero-hour contracts

Chapter 4

Tackling Government Waste, Lowering Taxes

A vote for UKIP is a vote in favour of allowing more of us to keep more of our own money by cutting income tax, taking everyone on minimum wage out of tax altogether, and abolishing inheritance tax and road tolls. It is a vote to stop wasteful government spending and vanity projects, to grow Britain's wealth through extracting shale gas, and develop a stricter, but fairer welfare system.

The UK's tax regime is notoriously complex. In 2009 Britain won the dubious honour of being home to the longest tax code in the world – the handbook of tax legislation ran to 11,520 pages, more than double the number from twelve years previously.[45] As Gordon Brown loved tinkering with obscure and detailed rules, perhaps this should not surprise us.

There is a tax on just about everything it seems: income tax, VAT, inheritance tax, stamp duty, council tax, business rates, betting tax, fuel duty, landfill tax, car tax, air passenger duty, the congestion charge, capital gains tax – the list must be endless but quite where it ends is beyond most of us. According to the TaxPayers' Alliance (TPA), which does keep track of these things, our tax regimes

---

45   Office of Tax Simplification.

change so much and so frequently that the 2013 Autumn Statement by the Chancellor included the 509th tax rise and the 209th tax cut of this parliament alone. Osborne is hardly restoring the tax system's 'reputation for simplicity, stability and predictability' as the 2010 Conservative Party manifesto promised.[46]

UKIP is firmly of the opinion that we all pay too many taxes, and that many of us also pay too much. High taxes stunt economic recovery by discouraging inward investment to Britain and divesting us individually of our incentives to work and invest. UKIP is also convinced the taxes we pay are too often wasted on unnecessary public sector spending. The TPA's *Bumper Book of Government Waste* claims £120 billion a year is 'squandered on useless projects' and that we pay over the odds for everything from salaries and bonuses for public sector staff to unnecessarily and expensively outsourced services and facilities. The TPA puts the estimate of this waste at £4,500 for every family in Britain.

Clearly this money could be used to provide a better standard of living, and this is Nigel Farage's ultimate aim as leader of UKIP: 'I want to give millions of ordinary people and families in this country the opportunity to live a better life and do better,' he told the BBC's Andrew Marr. 'What we want to do is genuinely address the cost of living and to address social mobility.'[47]

The state of the economy

Although the UK economy is currently among the fastest growing in the developed world, it does not feel like it for most of us. One reason for this is that our population has also increased, so we all get a smaller slice of the pie. But it is also because family income is still squeezed by the cost of living crisis as a result of much higher food, fuel and transport bills. While wages rose by 0.3 per cent

46   p.16.
47   1 June 2014.

between May 2013 and May 2014, inflation was running at 1.9 per cent. It will be a long time before we feel comfortably well-off as a nation again.

Unemployment has fallen to an apparent six-year low as of July 2014,[48] but how reliable are these figures? Unemployment figures are calculated by taking the number of people claiming Jobseeker's Allowance (JSA) into account, but we know thousands of JSA claimants have had their benefits stopped following a period of radical changes to the welfare system.[49] When people cannot find full-time work they will also accept part-time work, perhaps even work on zero-hour contracts simply because it is all they can get. Still more will be self-employed people who overall are on much lower incomes. And even without taking any of this into account, we still have more than two million people unemployed in Britain, and, shockingly, half of them are under the age of twenty-five.

Despite tax rises and government cuts, our national debt is still rising. George Osborne inherited a record level of debt from Gordon Brown in 2010 and promised to reduce it, but he is in fact on course to have increased that debt by 50 per cent by the time of the 2015 election.[50]

Yet despite this gloom, and the pressure on budgets, the government has kept our overseas aid budget pegged religiously to 0.7 per cent of GDP – more than £11 billion a year. Our contribution to the EU has risen dramatically. All three old political parties are committed to excessive spending on vanity projects such as the HS2 rail link. Meanwhile, the government is making sweeping

---

48 Office for National Statistics.

49 In North Staffordshire alone, for example, the Citizen's Advice Bureau in Stoke-on-Trent revealed 4,223 claimants at Hanley job centre alone had their benefits stopped between November 2012 and December 2013, as reported in the Stoke Sentinal, 28 July 2014.

50 Public sector net debt in May 2010 was £903 billion; in January 2014 it was £1,240 billion.

cuts to pay for all this, and hard-pressed taxpayers are understandably not best pleased.

As if the pressures on family budgets and the huge burden of existing taxes is not enough, we face the constant threat of new taxes to fill the revenue's coffers. The Labour Party wants a rise in corporation tax, fuel duty and national insurance, and has resurrected plans to introduce a 15 per cent 'death tax' to pay for people's care in their old age, a move backed wholeheartedly by shadow Health Secretary Andy Burnham. Labour is also talking about a graduate tax. The Tory–Lib Dem coalition is now seeking to collect inheritance tax even before we are dead, and the Mayor of London Boris Johnson wants to introduce an additional levy on diesel cars. There is talk of a 'sugar tax', and the EU wants to bring in a 'Robin Hood' tax on share and bond transactions which could wipe billions off our pensions. The Liberal Democrats are determined to push ahead with a 'mansion tax' on large properties, even though those living in them may be otherwise impoverished. A Labour Party councillor is urging her party to do the same – but to lower the threshold to homes worth just £400,000.[51]

Believing this is the people's money, not government money, UKIP wants to let us keep more of our own earnings, and so seeks a different route to jump-starting the economy. This starts with eliminating our contributions to the whole of the EU budget and axing red tape so businesses becomes more profitable; cutting government waste and excess spending; easing the pressure on the welfare system; and seeking a broader range of free trade deals worldwide. Letting hard-working families keep and spend more of their well-earned money themselves – rather than giving it to the government to waste – will lead to faster economic growth, more inward investment in Britain, more jobs and greater national prosperity.

---

51   Councillor Claire Reynolds speaking at an event held by Progress, a New Labour pressure group, reported in the *Sunday Express*, 10 August 2010.

Minimum wage? Why pay tax?

UKIP's firm pledge on income tax is a commitment to ensuring the lowest paid pay no tax at all. UKIP would take anyone working a normal week on the minimum wage out of tax altogether by aligning the tax-free personal allowance to the minimum wage. We believe this is only fair and ethical: if we deem a wage to be the minimum for which someone should be asked to work, the minimum they need to live on, why on earth should they pay any tax on it? It will also help incentivise people to get off benefits and get back to work.

UKIP would also like to see the top rate of tax cut from 45 per cent down to 40, and with a £45,000 threshold at which it begins to be paid. Middle-income earners are frequently in the treasury's sights when it comes to taxation and they are paying more now than they were when the current government came to power in 2010. The threshold is lower now than it was then.

Being in the 40 per cent tax bracket does not make you 'wealthy' as Labour seems to think when it talks about these taxpayers as being 'the richest in the country'.[52] Try getting a mortgage to buy even a small flat in London on £31,000 a year and you will soon see how someone on that income is by no means 'rich', especially if you have children to support.

Too many people are being pulled into the 45 per cent tax bracket – 400,000 middle-class professionals under the coalition says Nigel Farage:

> The top rate of tax was supposed to be for high earners. Now, in London and the south east, the top rate of tax has clawed in a lot of people who are far from what would be described as high earning. The numbers paying the top rate of tax has grown hugely under both of the past two administrations and we don't think that is reasonable.

---

52   Ed Balls speaking at a public meeting in Bedford, 29 July 2014.

Labour meanwhile has said they will increase this tax band to 50 per cent for the lifetime of the next parliament and the Lib Dems say they would keep it pegged at its current level.

What UKIP will *not* do is introduce a flat tax as was proposed in our 2010 manifesto. The idea to have a flat tax of 31 per cent and abolish national insurance was widely misunderstood at the time, mainly because opposition parties criticised the tax element of the policy while choosing to ignore the reference to NI which would have meant that no one would be worse off.

Killing off inheritance tax

Seven years ago, the Conservatives promised to abolish inheritance tax on all estates worth less than £1 million if they got into government, but quickly abandoned this pledge in the face of pressures from their Lib Dem colleagues who prefer to tax the rich. Now they have announced plans to stop legitimate tax planning schemes by insisting that in some cases death duties will have to be paid in advance, while savers and homeowners are still alive. Head of Policy Tim Aker MEP says:

> UKIP has consistently advocated the complete abolition of inheritance tax. Inheritance tax brings in under £4 billion – less than a third of what we spend on foreign aid. The super-rich avoid it, while modest property owners get caught by it. It hits people during a time of grief and UKIP will budget in its 2015 spending plans to completely abolish this unfair death tax.

Spotlight on local government spending

The local government gravy train is out of control. In 2011/12 at least 2,181 council employees received total remuneration in excess of £100,000. In 2012/13, 542 council employees received more than

£150,000 and of these, thirty-four were paid over £250,000. The council employee with the largest remuneration package in the UK in 2012/13 was David Crawford, the executive director of Social Care Services at Glasgow Council, who received £486,303, a figure that included a considerable redundancy package. The highest paid council chief executive not in receipt of one-off payments due to redundancy in the same year was Paul Martin, chief executive of Wandsworth Council, whose annual salary was £274,224, almost double what the Prime Minister is paid.[53]

Councils are also spending small fortunes on self-promotion and advertising, including 'propaganda rag' magazines. Some councillors are earning more than twice the average wage for what is intended to be a part-time role, staff are running up huge bills on council credit cards, and essential goods and services cost well over the odds because of poor procurement.

Meanwhile, council tax rises, fees for council services go up, more people find themselves having to pay care fees, and motorists are fleeced with spiralling parking charges and fines issued by over-zealous parking attendants. Too many local councils are taking the easy way out and, instead of cleaning up their own acts and operating more efficiently, they simply hike fees for residents. Often this is done as deliberate policy: a Labour council will purposely make life difficult for residents, for instance, so they can blame cuts made by a Conservative government in the hope this will improve their re-election chances next time around. Too often, party politics is put before people and before taxpayers. It is not how UKIP likes to operate.

UKIP would cut excessive allowances for councillors, slash inflated salaries for senior council staff, limit the number of highly paid council employees, abolish non-essential positions, cut advertising and PR budgets and be more rigorous in procurement, all with the aim of keeping council tax as low as possible.

---

53   Figures from the TaxPayers' Alliance.

We would also invest in partnership with the voluntary sector, because we believe community groups and volunteers are often better placed to run services and facilities than the state. By ensuring these groups are supported and empowered we will be able to achieve much more for our communities and often for less money too.

Abolishing road tolls and charges and cutting fuel duty

Other taxes in UKIP's sights are fuel duty, road tolls and congestion charging. Fuel duty is far too high and is holding the economy back, while toll roads have been described as 'nothing more than highway robbery' by UKIP Deputy Leader Paul Nuttall. 'Automatic number plate recognition cameras and automated tolling suites may be more advanced than pistols and a cry of "stand and deliver", but Dick Turpin would recognise it nonetheless,' he says. 'Tolling hits the less well-off disproportionately and should be scrapped for the benefit of all.'

Banishing the bedroom tax

UKIP would abolish the 'under-occupancy penalty', an extension of Labour's local housing allowance (2008) first piloted in 2001 under the auspices of Malcolm Wicks MP, then Secretary of State for Work and Pensions. UKIP considers it to be unfair and deeply upsetting for people to be forced out of their homes simply because they have a spare room for which they cannot afford to pay extra. UKIP councillors around the country have gathered stories of both hardship and stupidity around this tax: hardship because social housing tenants are told they must either pay extra or find a new, smaller home, but councils or housing associations are unable to find alternative accommodation for them; stupidity when councils have paid out thousands of pounds for homes to be adapted to accommodate disability, but then the residents are told they must leave. It does not free up housing, it just makes people in them poorer.

Scrapping green taxes

UKIP will also scrap the 'green taxes' which add enormously to the cost of heating and lighting our homes, a massive issue of huge concern for many people and which forced 2.28 million English households alone into fuel poverty in 2012 – that's 10.4 per cent of all households in England.[54] This is a national scandal and it is driven for the most part by the burden of EU climate and energy policy.

The EU is a keen supporter of so-called 'green' or 'renewable' energy such as wind, hydropower and solar power and it is demanding that 15 per cent of the UK's total energy consumption should come from such sources by 2020. The UK government's favoured source of renewable energy is wind power, hence why more and more wind farms are popping up all over Britain. However they are highly uneconomic. Taxpayers' money regularly subsidises wind farms that require gas powered back-up when the wind doesn't blow, which is often. On 21 December 2010, for instance, a time of year when you'd think it might be quite gusty, wind power made only a 0.04 per cent contribution to the UK's energy consumption[55] and even on an average night, the industry only runs at 13 per cent capacity.[56]

Meanwhile, at other times, there is too much wind and turbines have to be shut down. In 2011, seventeen wind farm operators were paid £7 million to shut them down on forty occasions between

---

54 Annual Fuel Poverty Statistics Report, 2014, Department of Energy and Climate Change.
55 'Electricity costs: The folly of wind-power', Civitas report by Ruth Lea January 2012.
56 'Characteristics of the UK wind resource: Long-term patterns and relationship to electricity demand' by Graham Sinden, Environmental Change Institute, Oxford University Centre for the Environment.

January and September because the wind was too strong for them
to cope with.[57]

Despite this failure, green taxes are added to bills to fund renewable energy projects such as building wind turbines, solar farms and
so on. The TaxPayers' Alliance estimates that green taxes and VAT
account for 11 per cent of a typical gas bill and 16 per cent of an electricity bill, adding £620 a year to a typical household's energy bill by
2020.[58] With all three legacy parties committed to investing in green
energy, things can only get worse without UKIP.

Energy spokesman Roger Helmer says:

> UKIP is not opposed in principle to renewables. Hydroelectricity, for
> example, is predictable, controllable and economic. But we are against
> widespread use of wind and solar, which offer an unpredictable and inter-
> mittent trickle of very expensive electricity, requiring 100 per cent back-up.
> These renewables undermine economic competitiveness, damage our
> economy and threaten security of energy supply. We have no problem
> with private companies investing their own money in renewables, if they
> can do so without subsidy.

The future lies in shale

Energy is in increasingly short supply and Britain urgently needs more
gas-fired capacity to plug the gap while new nuclear power stations are
built – UKIP believes nuclear power is a vital part of the energy mix.
North Sea gas is in decline and cannot be relied upon long term. The
answer to the supply shortage is shale gas, of which there is believed
to be a plentiful supply in the north west and the midlands.

The technique for extracting shale gas, fracking, is controversial,

---

57 'Wrecked by gales again as wind farms get £300,000 to switch off ... in high winds' by
    Tamara Cohen, *Daily Mail*, 6 January 2012.
58 'Green taxes to increase energy bills by a third by 2020' by Andrew Trotman and
    Andrew Oxlade, *Daily Telegraph*, 4 July 2013.

but then, the green lobby seems to be opposed to just about every viable energy technology. Various government investigations have concluded the process is safe and has recently re-opened bidding for fracking licences at various sites around the UK.

The technology could potentially reinvigorate rural economies as well as cut our gas bills. 'Shale gas has allowed the United States to turn from being a net importer of gas to a self-sufficient net exporter and no one talks about an energy crisis in the US any longer,' Paul Nuttall says. 'Shale gas has also allowed energy prices to fall by 30 per cent in some places in the US which has been a much-needed boost at a time of economic hardship.'

Up to 750,000 jobs have also been created through shale in America, and now India and China are pushing ahead with programmes to extract shale gas.

'Shale also offers a way of ensuring we are not reliant on politically unstable – and often bullying – countries for our oil and gas reserves,' says Nigel Farage, no doubt thinking of the recent issues with Russia and Ukraine, in which Russia has deliberately used gas supplies as a political weapon against its neighbours.

Significantly, UKIP would also harness the tax revenues from shale gas into a sovereign wealth fund to benefit Britain. Farage adds:

Unlike those blasted windmills which smoothly transfer money from the poor to the rich by means of subsidies and green levies, fracking would provide this country with energy and with money which UKIP proposes to put into a sovereign wealth fund, free from the greedy clutches of government departments. The revenues from North Sea oil went directly to the coffers of the Treasury, but UKIP would follow the example set by Norway where today their fund set up to invest revenues from oil and gas is worth around $750 billion, 150 per cent of the country's GDP.[59]

---

59 'It's the oil and gas stupid! Until we start fracking, Russia will always win, says Farage', *Daily Express*, 7 March 2014.

Paying for tax cuts

Tax cuts kick-start the economy, which in turn grows and delivers payback, but in the first instance they have to be paid for either by making cost savings or generating income. UKIP's 2015 manifesto will supply fully costed, peer-reviewed proposals for all policies suggested, but, meanwhile, here are some key areas the party will be seeking to cut in order to fund other manifesto commitments.

An end to government waste and vanity projects

Anyone who has worked in national or local government or even the public sector knows a huge amount of money is wasted. On 10 February, the TaxPayers' Alliance (TPA) claimed that the government wasted £120.4 billion in 2012/13, the equivalent of £4,560 per every household in the UK. This is a greater amount that the UK budget deficit and more than the GDP of New Zealand.

The TPA published a long list of just some of the ways in which politicians wasted our money that year, including:

- £22.5 billion in overpayments on public sector pay and pensions compared to the private sector
- £20.6 billion wasted on public sector fraud, according to the National Fraud Authority
- £1.2 billion spent on claims for clinical negligence in the NHS
- £1.6 billion cost of higher sickness levels in the public sector than in the private sector
- £1.1 billion on excessive subsidies to train operating companies
- £300 million wasted on unused and destroyed medicine in the NHS
- £1.4 million for Department of Work and Pensions software licenses for a cancelled project with £471,000 wasted on a single office left empty for eight months

- £342,000 for a Foreign Office-funded TV series with a production company that went bust
- £382,000 spent on hotel rooms booked for the 2012 Olympic Games that were left unoccupied

The government all too frequently behaves in a way which suggests it forgets this is taxpayers' money going down the drain. Far too much is wasted at local, national and European levels, and UKIP would get a grip on this and slash wastage.

Making welfare responsible

Britain spends approximately £208 billion on benefits every year. Of every £3 the government gets in revenue, nearly £1 is spent on welfare. While it might not feel like it if you are living on them, if you are on welfare in Britain, you are actually among the wealthiest 14 per cent of people on the planet, according to Mark Littlewood of the Institute of Economic Affairs,[60] yet almost half of all benefit payments go to people who have never actually paid into the pot: only 43 per cent of welfare benefits are made to people who have contributed to the system by paying national insurance.[61]

The system needs reform. While no one would deprive those who have fallen on hard times of benefits, they should be a safety net for the needy, not a bed for the lazy. Unlike the old parties who aim to cut the welfare budget across the board, UKIP intends to make savings through stopping the abuse of the welfare system. There are some changes which can be made very quickly outside the EU, notably a tightening up of the rules on paying benefits to migrants who have not contributed to the UK economy or who are acting in a way which most reasonable people would think is abusing the system. For instance, it was recently revealed that there are thousands of migrants who

60 Speaking at UKIP's Young Independence conference in 2013.
61 Figures from the House of Commons Library 2012/13.

are claiming sick pay despite living in another country,[62] and some 20,400 migrant families receive child benefits totalling £30 million a year for children who do not actually live in Britain.[63]

It also costs £1.7 million a month to house migrant families in Britain, more than 2,000 of whom are living here rent-free,[64] arguably a sign of the huge burden uncontrolled immigration has added to our country's limited housing stock, given the long waiting lists.

Meanwhile, more than 370,000 migrants who were admitted to Britain to work, study or go on holiday are now claiming out-of-work benefits here, according to official figures compiled for the first time in 2011 using records held by the UK Border Agency, Department for Work and Pensions and HM Revenue and Customs. It is not just non-working migrants who add to our tax and welfare bills: those who are working in Britain claim £5 billion a year in total tax credits, figures from HMRC and the Migration Advisory Committee show, as foreign nationals make up 17 per cent of Britain's 2.45 million child tax credit claimants.

UKIP would put a stop to this, ensure that any kind of in- or out-of-work benefits are only available for those who have lived here for over five years, and prioritise social housing for people whose parents and grandparents were born locally. This would make a huge dent in Britain's annual welfare bill and deter from coming to Britain those who are able to support themselves and their families.

HS2: the EU vanity project that UKIP will ditch

This proposed new high-speed rail link will cut just twenty minutes off a journey from London to Leeds. UKIP says there is no money

---

62   'Lost the plot: Outrage as thousands of migrants living abroad are still claiming sick pay' by Giles Sheldrick, *Daily Express*, 6 June 2014.

63   'This Polish boy lives in Warsaw … So why do WE pay his child benefit?' by Sue Reid, *Daily Mail*, 29 July 2014.

64   '£1.7 million a month to house migrant families' by Anil Dawar, *Daily Express*, 25 July 2014.

to pay for it, there is no proof it will benefit anyone except a small few. It will bring devastation to towns, villages and ancient woodlands along the route which will be destroyed.

Originally estimated to cost £43 billion, that figure was upped to some £70 billion, but these estimates are already proving to be a very sick joke: Department for Transport's (DfT) spending to the end of February 2014 reveals that the Whitehall-run firm set up to manage the project – HS2 Ltd – has already overshot its allocated £101 million consultancy budget by £87 million for four lots of professional services contracts. The total spend on consultants alone so far totals £188 million, 86 per cent over the most recent budget.[65]

The salaries of officials working on the controversial scheme have also been called into question, most notably by UKIP's transport spokeswoman, Jill Seymour MEP, who has been horrified to discover as many as thirty new members of staff will be paid more than the Prime Minister, who gets £142,500 a year. She says:

> It is obscene to be spending so much money in the first place on HS2, which will be of little or no benefit to the majority of people in our country. To then start employing bureaucrats on these fat-cat salaries, at a time when the UK still has to borrow huge sums to make ends meet, is obscene. It is rubbing salt into the wounds.

UKIP believes HS2 is a 'white elephant' which should be scrapped, with the budgets transferred into improving the existing rail and public transport infrastructure to benefit far more people.

All these initiatives combined will help create a fairer, more self-sufficient Britain, in which the government takes first responsibility for fiscal prudence, invests in technologies to grow the economy and provide for her citizens, then gives back in a way that rewards working people and is fair to those who fall on hard times.

---

65 *Building Magazine*, 16 May 2014.

Vote UKIP to:

- Cut income tax
- Take those on minimum wage out of tax altogether
- Abolish inheritance tax
- Reduce waste in local and national government
- Keep council tax as low as possible
- Cut fuel duty and scrap road tolls and charges
- Axe the bedroom tax
- Scrap green taxes
- Extract shale gas to cut fuel bills and create a sovereign wealth fund
- Cut the welfare bill in a way that is fair
- Stop vanity projects such as HS2

Chapter 5

Ethical Foreign Policy and Trade, Not Aid

A vote for UKIP is a vote for trade, not aid: an opportunity to make rigorous cuts to the foreign aid budget and support developing nations by boosting their ability to grow their own economies, not undermine them with handouts. It is also a vote to stop sending aid to corrupt countries with poor human rights records; a vote against being dragged unnecessarily into foreign wars where no pressing national interest is at stake; for keeping an independent foreign policy; and in support of Britain taking her fair share of refugees from war-torn nations.

Despite the fact the European Union itself does not have the legitimacy to be framing a foreign policy, we are seeing one, aren't we? Because there was a European summit that took place in Brussels this week. Now it seemed at that summit they couldn't agree much about what to say about Russia and the situation in South Ossetia, but there is one thing they all agree on, that all the European leaders agree on – David Cameron agrees on it and the Lib Dems agree on it – they all agree that the European Union and NATO should continue to expand to the east and that we should take in the Ukraine and Georgia as members of both organisations, and I think this is one of the most dangerous foreign policy developments I've seen in my lifetime ... I'm not defending what is going on in South Ossetia at the moment but what I'm saying is, to expand the EU, and expand NATO

and to take in Ukraine, to take in Georgia, would be a provocative act in
what is an unstable country and it would be absolute madness.

These were Nigel Farage's words at UKIP's autumn conference all the
way back in 2008, before the current crisis in Ukraine. What prophetic
words: he could see the writing on the wall and, sadly, he was right.

The EU: troublemaker, not peacemaker

The EU frequently argues for its existence by saying it has prevented
wars being fought on European soil and will keep the peace in the
future. In a recent debate in the European Parliament to commem-
orate 100 years since the outbreak of the First World War, speaker
after speaker peddled the line that 'nation states need to be done
away with, because nation states create wars' which, presumably,
the EU never would. UKIP Deputy Leader Paul Nuttall's response?
'Complete tosh – and they know it.'

He says he nearly fell off his chair when Jose Manuel Barro-
sso (at the time President of the EU Commission) referred to the
Great War as 'Europe's first civil war', a statement both insulting
and factually incorrect given the heroic and sacrificial role played
by troops from South Africa, India, Australia, New Zealand and the
USA – not to mention the historical idiocy of forgetting all previous European conflicts.

He says:

> The EU is what I call a 'false state' which is when people who don't share
> culture, language or history are forced together without being asked first.
> The Soviet Union ... was a false state. And false states only ever end in one
> of two ways – in peaceful divorce like Czechoslovakia or bloody war like
> Yugoslavia. The EU is trying to rewrite history to justify its own existence
> and, rather than preserving peace, it is dragging the peoples of Europe
> into a potentially dangerous future.

Nigel Farage later described the EU as 'having blood on its hands' with regard to its involvement in Ukraine, and was rounded on by a pro-European media. 'But you don't need to be a massive Putin fan to acknowledge that Farage has a point – it was the EU that provoked this crisis in Ukraine, not the Russians,'[66] argued journalist James Delingpole. 'The short-sightedness of the EU's plan to expand its empire right to Russia's borders ... appears completely to have overlooked how the Russians might feel about having a neighbour and trading partner dragged from their sphere of influence without so much as a by-your-leave.'

Delingpole continued:

> Putin hinted as much to Baroness Ashton – the former Campaign For Nuclear Disarmament campaigner who in 2009 was promoted way above her pay grade to the position of the EU's High Representative of the Union for Foreign Affairs and Security Policy – when he warned her in January not to make any more appearances on the barricades in Kiev with anti-Yanukovych protestors. When the EU's leaders ignored Putin's heavy hints that Ukraine was a problem best sorted out locally, the Russian intervention was inevitable.

EU foreign policy: where vanity takes the place of reason

UKIP is in no doubt that the EU is anything but a force for peace. Even putting aside the internal conflict it has precipitated in those countries suffering from the collapse of the euro – riots in Greece and Portugal for instance – at a supra-European level the intensifying pursuit of expansion and dominance is clearly becoming a force for ill.

Nigel Farage says:

---

66 'Nigel Farage is right: it was the EU, not Russia, that provoked the Ukraine crisis' by James Delingpole, *Breitbart News*, 28 March 2014.

We are seeing vanity take the place of reason in foreign policy and the result is to destabilise a whole series of countries to no positive effect that I can discern. It is not just the Ukraine. The civil war in Syria was made worse by EU leaders stoking the expectation of Western forces helping to topple the Assad dictatorship, despite the increasing dominance of militant Islamists in the rebellion. In the case of the Ukraine, Brussels has for many years been feeding an entirely unrealistic dream of a future as an EU member state and large net recipient of funds. This has encouraged brave young men and women in western Ukraine to rebel to the point of toppling a legitimate president and led to the utterly predictable debacle whereby Vladimir Putin has annexed part of the country and now casts a long shadow over hopes of genuine democracy in the rest of it. I do not support what Putin has done – of course I don't. But the approach of David Cameron, William Hague, Nick Clegg and other EU leaders has been disastrous. If you poke the Russian bear with a stick he will respond. And if you have neither the means nor the political will to face him down, that is very obviously not a good idea.

Enough is enough

The British public are fed up with being dragged into conflicts such as the illegal Iraq war, and especially so when there is no pressing national interest at stake. Our leaders may argue they seek the birth of a new peaceful democracy in these countries, but the bitter truth is that often, dictators often keep a lid on seething internal ethnic or religious conflict and, when that dictator is removed, there is no chance whatsoever for democracy. Despite evidence on our own European doorstep of this in Yugoslavia, for example, our political leaders seem determined they will not learn from history – either that or they are so egotistical that they believe they can succeed where others have failed.

When the USA backed the 'Mujahideen' against Russia in Afghanistan in the '80s and lavished those 'freedom fighters' with weapons, twenty years later they were forced to invade Afghanistan again; the Mujahideen had morphed into the Taliban and so the US had a fresh vipers' nest to deal with, only this time one that turned their own weapons against them. Did Britain or Europe learn even from this very recent history? No. Is Iraq a more peaceful place since we helped topple Saddam Hussein? No: barbaric terrorists of the vilest kind are running amok beheading, hanging and crucifying men, women and children in the name of a 'Caliphate,' or 'Islamic state'. Yet some of these despicable terrorists were once 'rebels' that the British government considered funding in order to overthrow President Assad in Syria. It was UKIP who launched the ultimately successful campaign against arming them, and UKIP who pushed the government into changing its mind when it refused to accept any refugees fleeing Syria. Now, hundreds of thousands more are fleeing what is being called a 'Christian holocaust' in Syria and Iraq; the numbers of casualties far, far higher than any claimed by Hussein or Assad. The Americans, meanwhile, are once again bombing the same terrorists they once supported.

If Britain's judgement has been appalling, the EU's has been even worse, yet it is frequently proposed that the EU should take responsibility for Europe-wide foreign policy and replace Britain and other national states on the UN Security Council, no doubt as a precursor to the development of a full EU army. This is provided for under the terms of the Lisbon Treaty (subject to a full member vote) and has been called for by senior figures such as the German Chancellor Angela Merkel and French President Nicolas Sarkozy as well as others, yet such a move is frequently – and somewhat bafflingly – denied.

In fact the EU already has a militarised 'rapid-reaction force', EUFOR, with 2,800 troops that have been mobilised in countries such as the Democratic Republic of Congo, Chad and the Central African Republic, as well as Gaza, and there is a clear appetite to go further. UKIP will have no truck with this. It is UKIP policy to maintain our own independent British Army, Airforce and Navy, insist on keeping absolute control of our own self-determining foreign policy, and retain our seats in NATO and on the UN Security Council. UKIP will also keep out of foreign wars unless there is a clear danger to British interests or a strong moral justification for intervention otherwise.

UKIP will also ensure it is not bolstering corrupt foreign regimes through our foreign aid programme; we have delivered far too much to countries with appalling human rights records with very little sense of where exactly the money is going or what it is being spent on. This must stop.

Trade, not aid

UKIP is committed to cutting the foreign aid budget, making aid-spending more accountable, and helping poorer countries to develop through trade, not aid.

Since the start of the economic crisis Britain has been the only G8 country to increase its international aid budget, which is pegged at 0.7 per cent of GDP. The Department for International Development (DfID) escaped the cuts faced by other departments – which according to the TaxPayers' Alliance would have been £1.9 billion if the budget had not been ring-fenced and cut in line with others. Moreover, our foreign aid budget, which already dwarfs the police budget, is set to increase to £12.6 billion by 2015, the equivalent of £500 a year in contributions from every household.

Perhaps we might not begrudge that. After all, most of us want to feel that our country is doing its bit, and so it should. But even if we do take that view, surely foreign aid must be about more than just appeasing our consciences, and we should be confident it is spent wisely and fairly?

Many of the countries we give donations to have foreign aid programmes of their own. Brazil, for instance, is funding AIDS and HIV anti-retroviral drugs in Mozambique. China also gets millions in handouts, despite holding £2 trillion in reserves in its own bank account and a programme of soft loans, debt cancellation and building projects which has funded projects in Ethiopia, Malawi and Tanzania. Over £2 million goes to Argentina, despite our less than friendly relations and the fact it is a G20 member. Although the government has announced plans to stop aid to India in 2015, for many years we have been sending aid there despite the country having nuclear weapons, its own aricraft carrier and a long-pursued space programme.[67]

Even when it is sent to more deserving countries, it is often difficult to assess precisely what aid achieves. Often the money is not properly subject to much in the way of scrutiny when it comes to results, which makes it easy for the unscrupulous to pocket it.

British aid money was used by the Ugandan dictator, President Yoweri Museveni, to buy a £30 million top-of-the-range Gulfstream G550 private plane in the same year ministers gave his poverty-ravaged country £70 million, for instance. Last year British taxpayers contributed to the £500 million handed out by the EU's External Action Service to Egypt to fight corruption, money which disappeared without trace.[68] You really couldn't make it up.

Over the past forty years, Africa has received $400 billion in aid, yet it is still the poorest continent in the world. While money may have helped alleviate some extreme and heartbreaking poverty in the short term, some projects are laughable. Why, for instance, are we spending £600,000 on children's TV in Kenya? Or £1.2 million towards the privatisation of utilities in Nigeria, together with another £80,000 on a study of the link between gender equality and growth in the country?[69] These are just politically correct vanity projects for Britain and inconsequential to most Africans.

---

67 Thanks to EU Parliament development advisor Michael McManus for this and other statistics in this chapter.

68 'Britain leads the way in foreign aid – unfortunately' by Ross Clark, *Daily Express*, 19 June 2013.

69 See *Daily Express* article, above.

There are also question marks over DfID's own spending. The department spends half a billion on consultants and £20 million for staff to stay in five-star hotels. When DiFD felt it needed to open a branch office in India with eighteen meeting rooms and 280 desks, the furniture bill alone came to £400,000.

Meanwhile, the poorest of us here in Britain are having to choose between whether to heat or eat. Half a million rely on food banks for basic sustenance and, as our national debt racks up and up, there is no money to deal with emergencies at home.

After Nigel Farage visited flooded villages in Somerset and Surrey early in 2014, he called for funds to be diverted from the foreign aid budget to help our own citizens who were suffering, a call that other party leaders dismissed but that got a lot of traction with the public. He wrote in the *Daily Express*:

> I know the fact that Britain's own Disasters Emergency Committee has ruled out a fundraising appeal for British floods victims has stuck in the craw of many of you. I feel exactly the same way. It is a sad moment when even our leading charities need reminding that charity should begin at home ... here in Britain just a few weeks' worth of the international aid budget spent on the home front could make a massive difference.[70]

UKIP believes the foreign aid budget needs to be flexible, rather than pegged unswervingly to a percentage of GPD, and that Britain's needs should come first so we can cope better with our own disasters such as flooding. We would not stop all foreign aid, but we would cut the budget so wealthier countries with their own aid and space programmes or those countries that had misused our aid, or used it for propaganda purposes, would no longer get handouts. We would also stop aid to countries with poor human rights' records, including those who deny rights to lesbian, gay, bisexual and transgender people.

---

70 'Let charity begin at home with a civil defence corps' by Nigel Farage, *Daily Express*, 14 February 2014.

Foreign aid spend under a UKIP government would be far more accountable and be limited to emergency relief and long-term projects such as vaccination programmes that have clear, achievable goals and are targeted to combat specific issues. We would also aim to invest in trade with developing nations in preference to giving handouts to develop their economies and ultimately their own self-sufficiency.

The billions we currently spent on foreign aid could be spent much more wisely, more ethically, and certainly not in the arbitrary way it is at present, which too often sees a transfer of wealth from poor people in the UK to rich dictators in other countries. UKIP's solution of trade, not aid, will reap far more dividends in the longer term and is, we believe, an altogether better approach.

Vote UKIP to:

- End participation in unnecessary wars where no British interests are threatened
- Stop propping up dangerous and divisive EU expansion projects
- Keep our own British armed forces
- Keep our seats on the UN Security Council and NATO
- Take our fair share of refugees
- Make rigorous cuts to the DfID spending and reasonable cuts to the foreign aid budget
- Stop aid to countries with poor human rights records
- Support developing nations with a 'trade, not aid' policy wherever possible

Chapter 6

Investing in the NHS

A vote for UKIP is a vote for an efficient, affordable, world-class NHS, free at the point of need. It is a vote to invest in hospital-based nurse training and real doctors not spin-doctors. It is a vote to scrap hospital parking charges, restore free eye and dental checks, and abolish costly, damaging EU directives.

Not to put too fine a point on it, the NHS is at breaking point. Possibly the most beloved post-war institution in Britain, our rapidly growing, ageing population which suffers increasingly from chronic diseases are putting crippling pressure on NHS finances, meaning it is now critically over-stretched. There is not enough money, there are not enough doctors and neither is the culture one that will allow the NHS to continue to deliver.

Interference from politicians is possibly all the NHS has suffered a surfeit of. Kicked around like a political football since it was launched in 1948, it has been badly battered and bruised by endless reorganisations and a top-down approach which has compromised patient care by putting targets before patients.

New governments will always try to leave an indelible mark on the NHS because they want to 'claim' it as theirs and prove only they are sensible and reliable custodians. 'You can't trust the Tories on the NHS' Labour sneers, wilfully forgetting their own appalling record.

Labour and Tories: both have failed the NHS

Instead of cherishing the NHS and holding it up as a beacon to the world, both the Conservatives and Labour have squabbled over it like spoilt children and ultimately, through their failed and myopic policies, brought it to the brink of ruin.

Financially, their management has been disastrous. Under the 1997–2010 Labour government, massive NHS spending projects were drawn up to boost poll ratings and win elections. They were paid for by reckless private finance initiatives (PFIs) that threw future generations into hock. Hospitals were built on debt, debt that was charged at credit card rates.

In total, Labour authorised £70 billion worth of loans which are costing at least £300 billion in repayments. The NHS shoulders one third of this. Now, unable to pay their debts, hospitals are forced to cut jobs and frontline services.

Juicy service contracts worth billions have been given to private companies. The EU Directive on Public Procurement (aka the NHS Act 2006) made it easy for huge corporates to take over from local businesses. The exchequer is currently looking at having to plug a £2 billion black hole in NHS finances, having already given A&E a £550 million bailout. No one even questions what this bailout money will buy; this is simply monopoly money dished out to a monopoly provider because of government failure.

After promising faithfully ahead of the 2010 election that there would be 'no top-down re-organisation of the NHS', David Cameron set about doing exactly that, at huge cost and with endless disruption to healthcare workers who were just getting to grips with the previous re-organisation. Tory reforms have cost billions: redundancy payments alone have totaled £1.6 billion since 2010. Louise Bours, UKIP's health spokeswoman, says these are gilt-edged golden handshakes that cost £108 million more than they should have – enough money to hire over 7,500 extra nurses:

> It is the public who employ the managers and if the government consulted
> them, they would find we want as much money to go on frontline ser-
> vices as possible, and as little as possible on redundancy packages. I can't
> imagine a hospital porter or a cleaner being given anything over the legal
> requirement, so why should some executive who doesn't go anywhere near
> patients? The NHS top brass need to remember who they work for – us.

Of those laid off, 4,000 have also been re-employed by the NHS since
and many more may well have been re-hired as consultants on far
higher salaries or daily rates.

Now, Ed Miliband says he will reverse Tory reforms.[71] What he
really means, of course, is another top-down shake up *disguised* as
repealing coalition legislation. So the political football game will continue with the losers, once again, being the NHS and the patients.

Labour threw money at the NHS with no appreciable improvement in standards. Why would there be? Spending in itself is not
and never can be a health outcome but, my goodness, the soundbite
'we're investing in the NHS' delivers politically.

An £11 billion failed NHS IT project was finally scrapped in 2013,
having been criticised from the outset as flawed. When Labour came
into power in 1997, spending on NHS managers totalled £130 million.
By 2010, this had spiralled to over £1 billion, an increase of 450
per cent. This excess spending has continued under the Conservative and Liberal Democrat coalition which has also increased NHS
budgets but, without tackling the enormous amount of waste, that
does nothing for patient care: 1,129 unnecessary jobs in areas such
as public relations, equality and diversity, energy and sustainabil-
ity, EU and 'green' staff, for instance. Money spent on spin-doctors,
rather than real doctors, has cost taxpayers over £46 million, money
that could have paid for 1,662 full-time nurses.[72]

---

71   Speaking to the BBC *Marr* programme, 27 July 2014.
72   Freedom of Information requests to every NHS organisation in the UK made by the Tax-
     Payers' Alliance although likely to be an underestimate given some trusts did not respond.

However, instead of abolishing the non-jobs introduced by Labour and investing the savings in responding to the shortage of trained medics which UKIP would do, the current government instead decides it would be a good idea to cut the budget supporting medical school places to save money. Utter madness.

Many more billions are wasted on procurement processes that would be considered a joke in the private sector. 'The level of waste around procurement is staggering, simply staggering,' says UKIP's Stephanie McWilliam, a radiographer for thirty years who then worked for the Department of Health and in healthcare management. She knows the lie of the land:

> Budget holders are so terrified of getting their budgets cut the following year that they deliberately overspend so they can argue they are underfunded. Then the competitive tender processes are incredibly complex and effectively mean larger companies with lobbying power get disproportionate amounts of business. More cost-effective SMEs [small and medium enterprises] that would cost the NHS less just can't compete. It is a big pharma marketing directors' dream: the NHS will pay £43 for a drug that's available over the counter for just £2.50.

Time to put patients first

Patients in our hospitals are dehydrated and malnourished because they are not being fed properly; hospital infections previously unheard of are now a major problem; 13,000 unnecessary deaths in just fourteen NHS trusts alone, with the Mid Staffordshire NHS trust scandal, in which former health secretaries Andy Burnham and Alan Johnson ignored eighty-one requests for a public inquiry in the two years after it was first warned of poor NHS care, being the worst example of inexcusably poor care.[73] That our hospitals can become

---

73 'Mid Staffs: Labour Government ignored MP requests for public inquiry into deaths' by Rowena Mason, *Daily Mail*, 17 February 2013.

inhospitable is the legacy of political interference in the NHS by Members of Parliament who have no experience of actually working in the health service. As surgeon Jon Stanley explains:

> The last sixty years has seen a growing divide between political 'experts' who have not held the hands or looked into the eyes of the sick and the desperate, and the healthcare workers and patients on the receiving end of their policies. As it becomes more and more about vote-winning targets, each new generation of healthcare workers becomes a little more dehumanised and less professional as procedures, objectives and measurable outcomes are put above individual patient advocacy.

Nowhere is this seen more clearly than in the GP's waiting room – if you can get a seat, that is. Idiotic Labour policies have seen doctors paid more for doing fewer hours and being able to opt out of weekend and out-of-hours cover, so getting an appointment has never been more difficult. The Royal College of GPs (RCGP) reports surgeries are turning away millions of patients due to a 'lack of investment in general practice'[74] and says that by 2015 patients in England will fail to get a GP appointment more than 51.3 million times, while fifty million more of us will have to wait over a week to see our GP or practice nurse. This is a crisis in primary care and one that has serious knock-on effects on A&E departments, because people with minor ailments who should go to see their GP can't get an appointment so go to hospital instead and clog up the system. This problem is bad enough but then, thanks to more stupid targets, if the not seriously ill fail to be seen within four hours at A&E, they are admitted into hospital, or the hospital concerned will be fined. Bed shortages mean hospitals are regularly and unnecessarily fined because of this. The cost to each hospital can run into the millions.

Andy Burnham MP, the shadow Secretary of State for Health,

---

74 RCGP press release issued 28 July 2014.

proposes to solve this problem with a commitment to ensuring anyone can see their GP within forty-eight hours. Again, it is just politicking. How will he ensure that with a national GP shortage? Yet another misconceived target from Labour that could lead to a Mid Staffordshire-style scandal in primary care as appointments are compressed and cancers missed and yes, GPs rather than thought-less politicians blamed.

EU interference: the straw that breaks the camel's back

'There is nothing in existence that is so bad, so incompetently run, so hopelessly inept, that a new EU directive cannot come along and make it even worse ... The EU has set the NHS on a course that is heading straight for an iceberg,' said consultant medical oncologist, Professor Angus Dalgleish, at the UKIP conference in 2013.

The consequences of EU directives cause colossal problems for health services. For example, the EU clinical trial directive which was brought in to harmonise clinical research has destroyed academic medicine in this country, a field in which we were world leaders. Before this directive came into force, we could trial cheap, effective drug combinations at minimal cost in the UK, but now academics have to find at least £2 million for even the simplest trial.

The EU working time directives, which limit the hours people can work in a week, have also taken their toll. The Royal College of Surgeons' outgoing president, Professor Norman Williams, called them no less than a 'straitjacket', damaging training and professional behaviour.

While no one wants to be treated by a doctor who has been working long shifts with no sleep, the NHS is struggling to run a safe service on an EU-engineered staff shortage. The 48-hour working week restrictions introduced under European law in August 2009 also push up spending on locum doctors, especially in hospitals providing 24-hour acute care. Meanwhile the system whereby surgeons are used to train up new specialists out of usual working hours has been destroyed.

The Royal College of Surgeons (RCS) commissioned research into this issue and subsequently revealed that 80 per cent of consultant surgeons and two-thirds of surgical trainees said patient care had deteriorated under the directive. Sixty-five per cent of trainees said their training time had decreased, while 41 per cent of consultants and 37 per cent of trainees reported 'inadequate handovers'.

John Black, President of the Royal College of Surgeons, said:

> To say the European working time regulations have failed spectacularly would be a massive understatement. Despite previous denial by the Department of Health that there was a problem, surgeons at all levels are telling us that not only is patient safety worse than it was before the directive, but their work and home lives are poorer for it.[75]

The RCS survey painted a picture of a horribly overstretched NHS with patients being increasingly assessed only by junior members of staff or routinely passed between many different doctors with varying levels of experience, often with unsafe, inadequate or no handover procedure. Senior surgeons, under pressure to get through operating lists, are now operating alone, causing a critical shortage of capable, skilled surgeons in the future. If students cannot learn and be supervised on the job, then the future for the NHS looks very bleak indeed.

NHS: the National or the International Health Service?

Conservatives, Labour and the Lib Dems are also in complete denial about the long term impact of immigration on our health services. The NHS is funded by tax, and so the ability to fund it depends on two

---

75   Press Release issued by the Royal College of Surgeons, 1 August 2010.

key principles being met: one, there is full or near-full employment, and two, there is control over our borders. The NHS developed outside the social insurance model primarily because our economy was strong and we are on an island. Mass migration and our EU membership has changed that landscape completely.

It is impossible to have a serious debate about the future of the NHS, or plan for future service delivery, without tackling the issue of immigration. 'The freedom to move from one country to another is great in principle', says Dalgleish, 'but in reality when one country provides everything free at the point of service including treatments unavailable in many countries, including EU countries, then demand can quickly outstrip the ability to provide.'

Foreign born mothers now account for one in four births, a situation which contributes to the fact there is not a maternity unit in the country that is not operating over capacity. Serious diseases such as tuberculosis have been re-introduced to Britain, and patients with poor English language skills require longer appointments, which puts additional pressure on time and resources. Yet at the moment, for reasons the Department of Health has never satisfactorily explained, all overseas visitors using British health services are granted an NHS number, which can translate seamlessly into expensive, long-term hospital care. 'A patient does not need to be ordinarily resident in the UK to be eligible for NHS primary care,' says the rulebook. 'Overseas visitors, *whether lawfully in the UK or not*, are eligible to register with a GP practice.' The Department of Health has helpfully advised GPs that it could be a violation of a patient's human rights to ask them for identification at the time of registration. The result is chaos: costs are supposed to be recovered from overseas visitors, but the fact they have an NHS number means NHS administrators are totally reliant on the goodwill of overseas visitors. As UKIP's Tim Aker MEP points out: 'Many hospitals are overburdened with long waiting times and do not want to act as immigration officials while the NHS is already buckling under the weight of administration.' The Department of

Health estimates 60 per cent of health costs to foreign visitors are never paid back. That's about £2 billion every year.

Health tourism is a growing problem and it is costing taxpayers substantial sums of money. While in an ideal world we would want the world's poor to enjoy the same standard of treatment we have, opening our NHS up to the world is not a sustainable way to achieve this goal.

How will UKIP save the NHS?

Under a UKIP government, the overwhelming bulk of healthcare budgets would be shifted to delivering frontline patient care. We would abolish the 'non-jobs' that have resulted either from our EU membership or political vanity and spend money on real doctors, not spin-doctors and unnecessary management.

UKIP would also restore free eye and dental checks because they pick up some very serious illnesses early on. These can then be treated at much lower cost and with far better outcomes as a result of early diagnosis, making savings in the longer term.

GP surgeries would open at least one evening a week to ease demand for appointments and help those who work during the day. Traditional training and nursing would also be restored: there is absolutely no need for all nurses to go to university and UKIP would bring back hospital-based training which concentrates on the practicalities of doing the job and delivering compassionate patient care. State-enrolled nurses from non-academic backgrounds can be trained in local colleges in half the time at a third of the cost of staff nurses. It works in Australia and New Zealand and used to work here. There is no reason why it could not work again.

The NHS will be free at the point of delivery but only to UK-born residents and those who have contributed to Britain as taxpayers for a five-year period (excluding emergency treatment which would be available freely to all). Under our plans, migrants would have to provide proof of private health insurance and submit insurance details when they register with a GP. This would be a simple and effective way of ensuring healthcare is available to everyone who comes here but closes the system to abuse. This could be done centrally by NHS England and the devolved health services so frontline staff can focus on delivering care and not have to act as informal immigration officers.

UKIP would also scrap hospital parking charges which are just an unfair tax on the sick and those who visit them.

The NHS has been messed about enough: UKIP would not reverse the coalition's reorganisation but it would streamline the Department of Health, invest in patient-centred frontline care, make NHS bodies more accountable to local people, and create an affordable, world-class health service of which Britain can be proud.

Vote UKIP to:

- Keep the NHS free at point of delivery
- Scrap hospital parking charges
- Stop the abuse of health tourism – foreign patients must pay
- Put patients first by investing in real doctors, not spin-doctors
- Bring back compassionate, vocational, hospital-based training for nurses
- Restore free eye and dental checks
- Axe failing, surplus NHS management
- Scrap EU health service directives
- Open GP surgeries in the evening and invest in primary care

Chapter 7

Putting British Farmers and Fishermen First

A vote for UKIP is a vote to remove the United Kingdom from the destructive Common Fisheries Policy to secure a future for the British fishing industry, replenish depleted fish stocks and revive ports and fishing villages. It is a vote to replace the bureaucratic, wasteful Common Agricultural Policy with a new single farm payment scheme linked to environmental good practice, and for policies that improve the welfare of farm animals.

We have more mouths to feed than ever before in Britain and so our farming and fishing industries are vital. Supporting and developing them and ensuring a secure and environmentally sustainable supply of food for both the UK market and for export abroad is a top priority for UKIP, a party which has always backed British farmers and fishermen.

Both industries are currently in decline. In 1939 there were some 47,000 fishermen in full- or part-time work across the United Kingdom. By the time we joined the EU in 1973, that figure had already more than halved. Today, there are only around 12,000 people still left in the business.[76] Meanwhile, 4.5 per cent of the country's workforce was in the farming industry in 1939 but by 2000 this had fallen

---

76   UK Sea Fisheries annual statistics 2012.

to 1.3 per cent. Between 2012 and 2013 alone the total labour force on commercial holdings decreased by 3.6 per cent and now we have just 464,000 people working on commercial farms in Britain.[77] This decline means we now import 40 per cent of all our food[78] and this trend must be reversed if we are to avoid being exposed to volatile global food and animal feed markets which can push up prices dramatically for producers and consumers.

At the moment, the EU has complete control over both farming and fishing industries in the UK, and over all aspects of food law. This frequently leaves the government hamstrung when it comes to trying to get a better deal for the agricultural industry. While we cannot control bad weather, or completely eliminate disease or blight, or solve all issues regarding global economic pressures on food prices, UKIP is convinced farmers and fishermen have everything to gain by leaving the EU and the huge amount of bureaucracy and external pressures membership brings with it. UKIP has sound policies that will put British farmers and fishermen first and help secure a vibrant, thriving agriculture sector for Britain.

Rescuing Britain's fishing industry

The EU-imposed common fisheries policy (CFP) is a travesty which is decimating the British Fishing Industry and causing catastrophic environmental damage to our seas and fish stocks. It is so cack-handed it is difficult to know where to begin in exposing how nonsensical it is.

The CFP works on the principle that fish move across European waters so the whole of Europe should be treated as one fishery with universal rules over movement, control and regulation applying to all EU member nations equally. So, although 60 per cent of waters

77 DEFRA.
78 'Food Matters: Towards a Strategy for the 21st Century'.

in the EU are British and Irish waters, and despite the fact Britain provides three-quarters of the EU's fish stocks, we have lost control over both because of the CFP.

If you thought Gordon Brown selling off our gold was bad, this is worse. Under United Nations' rules we would have fishing rights within a 200 nautical mile limit, yet as EU members only the 12 miles extending around our shores can be considered UK sovereign waters in which we alone can fish. At least that is the theory: in fact, other EU countries can register fishing vessels too large for their own quotas as British and catch our fish *within* the 12-mile limit. Indeed, approximately one fifth of the 'British' fleet is now in foreign ownership and catches significant percentages of UK quotas.

It is important to note that there was no CFP until Britain and Ireland joined the EU. When we joined, we opened up our precious waters to fleets from other EU nations, fleets that had been built up in advance of our membership using EU funds and which then came in and wiped our seas clean.

The CFP has been an economic and social disaster for Britain. It has conspired to devastate the British fishing industry and our fishing ports and towns. We have lost thousands of boats and thousands of jobs since the '70s. Over-fishing by other EU countries in British waters has massively depleted our fish stocks and even supplies of Britain's favourite and once abundant fish, the cod, are now dangerously low. The damage done is so bad that the entire UK fishing fleet now runs at a loss, and the EU pays out some £1 billion in subsidies and other assistance for the commercial fishing industry every year.

The problem with quotas

Needless to say, the EU has also inflicted all manner of harmful directives on fishermen which have compounded the problem.

Fishermen are only allowed to land their allocated 'quota' of fish.

This quota dictates the size, species and numbers that may be caught. When fish are caught over-quota they must be discarded back into the sea. Discarded fish are almost always dead or dying as they have been crushed into a net and their swim bladder will have been ruptured by being dragged up from the seabed – the aquatic equivalent of 'the bends' or decompression sickness. It is estimated that in the North Sea alone around 800,000–900,000 tons of fish are discarded back into the sea every year.[79] The annual economic value of UK dumped fish is £130 million.[80]

The discard policy has understandably been the subject of much criticism and the EU plans to end it by 2015/16. However, the alternative is little if any better, and will only add to the rising costs faced by fishermen and therefore the consumer. In future, the whole catch will have to be landed, stored, and taken back to shore. Yet fishermen can only sell or receive subsidies for the official quota they catch and not the rest, which will not be allowed to go into the human food chain. Not only is this a waste of perfectly good fish, it means fishermen will be facing double the costs on each trip, as the hold will be filled up with both quota and discard, which will cut their profits.

Irresponsible 'one-size-fits-all' policies

Soon, the use of driftnets will be banned too, to avoid 'bycatch' – fish or other marine species caught unintentionally by the wide nets which hang down in the sea. The ban on driftnets in Mediterranean waters is understandable as they catch turtles, dolphins, whales and other protected species but in Britain the driftnet ban will cause unnecessary economic hardship for fishermen who use them successfully for catching herring and bass, for example, with no significant adverse environmental impact. This ban is a classic example of the EU's 'one-size-fits-all'

---

79   Figures from British Sea Fishing.
80   TaxPayers' Alliance.

approach to policy making which causes immense problems for those countries where one size most definitely will not fit all.

Meanwhile, as the EU frets about driftnets, it allows and even subsidises other controversial methods of industrial fishing such as deep-sea trawling which has led Stuart Agnew MEP to suggest the fish produced as a result should be labelled: 'Taken from the oceans along with other species that will become extinct as a result, with the unwitting connivance of the British taxpayer.'[81]

Among one of the most notorious fishing methods the EU is allowing is known as pulse beam fishing, which Dutch fleets are currently trialling. This essentially involves using electric nets to electrocute and catch species that live low on the seabed. Banned in China after it caused huge damage to the shrimp population and species such as crabs and starfish, fishermen working out of ports in Essex and Kent shake their heads in dismay at the Dutch insistence that pulse trawling is a clean, safe and environmentally responsible way to catch fish. In 2012, it emerged that British fisherman were increasingly bringing in masses of dead Dover sole and that the numbers of live and healthy flatfish had declined dramatically since pulse fishing began in the area.

In an article in the *Sunday Times*, Tom Brown, secretary of Thanet Fishermen's Association, said his members complained it was like 'fishing in a graveyard' after the pulse trawlers had been in the area. 'What they don't catch, they annihilate,' he said. 'Virtually everything is dead.' Another fisherman reported he had never seen anything like it in the thirty years he had been fishing in the area: 'I think the pulse is killing the food in the seabed. Three years ago I caught 40 tons of sole in those grounds in one year. It was the best year we've ever had. There is nothing there now that I can catch.' A third talked about how the area now 'stinks of dead fish'.[82]

---

81   Speech made in the European Parliament, Brussels, 17 June 2013.
82   'Zapped: Britain's Fishing Graveyard', *Sunday Times*, 24 June 2012.

Foreign fishing rights

The EU has also made fishing agreements with at least twenty non-EU countries. These include Iceland and Norway, who are paid to allow EU trawlers to fish in their waters. However, the vast majority of those countries with whom the EU has agreements are developing countries such as Mauritania, Madagascar, Mozambique, Angola, Gabon etc. So, having orchestrated the demise of our own fish stocks, the EU is now paying poor countries so fishermen can exploit theirs. Needless to say, the fish caught is mostly sold in Europe. In addition, the EU is funding the build of huge fishing vessels which could never fish in European waters as their catch capacity is so big they would use up their quotas very quickly. It is over-fishing on a massive scale. Surely serious questions have to be asked about the way in which the EU is plundering African waters?

Taking all this into account, you will no doubt be surprised by the way in which the EU commissioners' website describes the CFP:

> A set of rules for managing European fishing fleets and for conserving fish stocks. Designed to manage a common resource, it gives all European fishing fleets equal access to EU waters and fishing grounds and allows fishermen to compete fairly.[83]

It beggars belief.

What would UKIP do?

To replenish Britain's bounty of fish to its seas, and restore Britain's fishing industry, a UKIP government would withdraw immediately from the common fisheries policy and establish an 'exclusive economic zone' to take back our 200-nautical mile territorial waters as defined by the 1982 United Nations Convention on the Law of

---

83   http://ec.europa.eu/fisheries

the Sea. This would return £2.5 billion a year in fish sales to the UK economy and support our fishing industry for future generations.

We would abandon EU quotas, forbid discards and require all commercial species of fish caught, regardless of size or species, to be landed and recorded so the government could begin to determine how to manage the recovery of UK fishing grounds. All forms of industrial fishing which have caused a catastrophic decline in fish species will be banned.

To preserve and replenish fish stocks in over-fished areas, UKIP will establish a series of 'no-take zones' to allow fish to spawn and recover. These zones would be moveable in sequence so as not to be detrimental to the livelihoods of fishermen. Within the EU, we are utterly helpless when it comes to replenishing fish stocks as to introduce conservation measures would require the agreement of all twenty-eight members states.

Only through these measures, and by strengthening the UK's fishery protection resources to guard British fishing ground, can we begin to replenish fish stocks, revive our fishing towns and ports, and secure a future for British fishermen.

Remain in the EU and the CFP and sooner or later, having fish for supper may become a thing of the past. Even Maria Damanaki, the EU's maritime commissioner, admitted in 2011 that the CFP had pushed Europe's fish stocks to the brink of extinction, saying: 'We cannot afford business as usual ... because if we do our children will see fish, not on their plates, but only in pictures.'

Making farming fairer

Controls on pesticides, food labelling, strict veterinary and animal transport rules, electronic sheep identification, flawed water nitrates directives – the EU's clutches are as firm and immovable when it comes to farming as they are in any other area of British life. UKIP would like British farmers to prosper, free from unnecessary red tape and with domestic policies better designed for their specific circumstances.

A brief history: from 1972 through to 1984 the EU's Common Agricultural Policy (CAP) offered financial support to farmers far in excess of anything experienced previously. It paid subsidies to farmers based on high, guaranteed prices for unlimited quantities of agricultural products and ensured high tariffs on imports along-side subsidised exports. This pushed up food prices. Then in 1984 two bubbles burst showing farmers for the first time that the CAP could go wrong. Milk quotas were imposed overnight in a manner that was devastatingly unfair, and later, a monumental grain harvest threw the system into meltdown. The World Trade Organization put pressure on the EU to dismantle the system which created such high prices for consumers and since then farmers have faced CAP reform of unbelievable complexity as the EU struggles to find a common policy for all twenty-eight EU countries.

To reduce price distortion, the connection between payments and production was removed and replaced by a single farm payment (SFP) which subsidises farmers on a per-hectare basis on land kept in 'good agricultural condition'. With the accession of several very poor member states to the EU, states which receive more funds than they contribute, farmers are unlikely to get any increase in the SFP any time soon.

'To deny this brutal dynamic is to put the head in the sand and leave certain parts hellishly exposed,' says UKIP's agriculture spokes-man Stuart Agnew MEP. 'The realistic view is to acknowledge that any future CAP changes will imply less money and more red tape.'

Stuart is a real farmer. A former Norfolk county chairman of the National Farmers Union, he was also the Norfolk Delegate to the NFU HQ Council from 2000 to 2009, until he relinquished the posi-tion on being elected to the European Parliament. He currently farms near Fakenham, Norfolk, where he has 35,000 free range hens, 500 ewes and 400 acres of arable land.

'UKIP will offer a simple version of the SFP, delivering the equivalent cash to most farmers, but at about half the cost to UK taxpayers,' he says. 'DEFRA has spent eight years of blood, sweat and tears learning how to administer the single farm payment and this effort should not be wasted. It will just be a simplified scheme free from the burden of Brussels bureaucracy, cross-compliance measures and red tape.'

At the moment, for every pound that goes into UK agriculture from the CAP, the UK taxpayer has already contributed two as part of the payment it makes to the EU, so UKIP's policy is undoubtedly affordable. Significantly, it will also help achieve what policy makers in Europe say they want to achieve but cannot: it will promote family farms and smaller-scale production.

Currently, EU subsidies are production-based, so the more acres of arable land you cultivate, or the more animals you have, the greater the amount of SFP subsidy you receive. This contributes to the fact that it is, on the whole, small- and medium-sized farms that are disappearing in Britain while the number of larger, often more intensively farmed holdings are increasing. The system works against smaller food producers who would rather get a fair price for the food they produce and have a sustainable, profitable business rather than take subsidies or find additional work off their farms in order to make ends meet, as many now must.

So whereas the SFP under the CAP benefits large, already wealthy landowners more than it does the smaller farmer, UKIP's scheme, which proposes a SFP of £80 per acre for farms of up to 1500 acres, capped at £120,000 per annum, would help small family farms and support those who want to enter the farming industry. Our proposals would also encourage younger farmers who are leaving the industry to stay – in 2000, almost a quarter of farm holders were under forty-five years old but by 2010 that figure had dropped to just 14 per cent.[84] Given the tough, outdoor life famers face, we need to keep younger people interested and working in agriculture.

---

84 DEFRA.

The 900 or so farmers who currently receive over £250,000 a year in subsidies[85] may well complain about UKIP's policy, but Stuart Agnew points out they have several options:

> They can either decide to stand on their own two feet and farm the land and reap the rewards, or let it out to a smaller farmer who can then claim their own SFP on it. I see this as a much fairer system, one which does not just reward the already affluent farmer, but one which helps social mobility too by potentially releasing more land up to those who want to start up in farming. However, we would be very tough on those who might try to abuse the scheme by using professionals to create networks of companies and so on.

There would be no set-aside under UKIP's proposals. Set-aside is the EU's controversial policy of paying farmers *not* to cultivate land to reduce surpluses and maintain prices.

Our argument is that we need to farm land and any half-decent farmer will know when land needs to lie fallow for a while, he or she does not need to be paid to protect their own livelihood in the longer term.

Also, to qualify for UKIP's SFP, land must be farmed to what is known as Entry Level Stewardship (ELS) standards to ensure environmental accountability. This requires farmers to maintain hedges, ditches, grass verges etc. and so play a community role in maintaining pleasant surroundings for everyone in the countryside as well as managing farmland for its own sake.

'Our aim in UKIP is to give farmers freedom to farm without a lot of regulation and introduce tighter rules on food imports,' he says. 'We also want to let consumers decide what standards should apply to UK food production, say on GM crops, but we would make sure they applied to imported food too.'

---

85   TaxPayers' Alliance.

Strange new crops: wind turbines and solar panels

Where the EU's climate change policies meet agriculture, there is an opportunity for a 'scam of monumental proportions' which UKIP would stop, says Agnew. The push for renewable energy sources has led many farmers to diversify away from traditional arable or livestock farming and into wind or solar energy, despite the need for food, and therefore traditional farming, being higher than ever.

Agnew says:

> Farmers like it when they are paid huge subsidies to have wind turbines or solar panels on their land. Many of them still think that these subsidies come from the taxpayer. Actually, they don't. They come from electricity consumers, who may well be very poor, individually. So what we are seeing is a reverse of the Robin Hood principle. We are robbing the poor to pay the rich. It is absolutely disgraceful.[86]

Agnew gives another example of how madness results when the CAP meets EU climate change policy by talking about biofuels. 'Again, this takes good arable land out of food production at a time when it is most needed,' he says. 'EU subsidies are tempting the farmer in the next field to not grow wheat but to turn it into maize, which will be put into an anaerobic digester, which will be connected to an electricity grid so that maize will be removed from agriculture.'

He points out that he, as a poultry farmer, needs

> quite large quantities of electricity and I get a quarterly bill and on that electricity bill is a surcharge called a 'climate change levy'. This is the subsidy I have to pay to the man or the firm in the next field to make

---

86 Stuart Agnew MEP speaking at a European parliamentary press conference with fellow members of the Agriculture and Rural Development Committee in Brussels, 2 December 2012.

his electricity competitive. It causes me an increase in my wheat price, because there is less about, and an increase in my electricity price. Then, if my business is still profitable enough to pay tax, what happens to that tax? It is handed to the farmer with the anaerobic digester as a single farm payment. I have four words to say: How mad is that?

Cutting red tape

UKIP wants to have a serious look at regulation on UK agriculture. 'Our premise will be one of "risk" as opposed to "hazard",' says Agnew.

Nitrate-vulnerable zones, the electronic identification of sheep, pesticides, waste, fallen stock burial, white asbestos cement sheets and BSE measures will all come into this, and significant de-regulation is achievable. However, the appalling incidence of serious accidents on farms, associated with the operation of machinery or falling from heights requires government involvement in helping the industry find solutions. Commodity futures trading will be encouraged and not restricted (or eliminated) by EU legislation. UKIP's practical energy policies will benefit the industry and the commercial growing of GM crops will be decided by a vote in the House of Commons, which will also regain control of food labelling.

On animal health issues, UKIP will be advised by relevant science and not pressure groups. We are, however, the only political party in Britain proposing and able to offer a ban on the export of live animals for slaughter. The damage to the rural economy will be marginal, but the improvement in welfare standards and the image of British farming will be greatly enhanced. UKIP will also impose far stricter controls on the import of bush meat from wild animals hunted in Africa, Asia, and South America which is frequently brought into the UK and sold illegally in butchers and markets. Not only does the trade have serious implications for the extinction of species, it can also pose a health risk and lead to outbreaks of serious diseases

– such as Ebola – and UKIP will not be bound by political correctness in tackling this dangerous trade.

Vote UKIP to:

- Leave the CFP and the CAP
- Take back control of our territorial waters
- Stop overfishing and replenish vital fish stocks
- End fish quotas and discards
- Clamp down on intensive fishing
- Back British farmers, including the smaller producer
- Support agriculture through a modified single farm payment
  scheme
- Get rid of unnecessary regulations that make farmers' lives
  more difficult
- Ban live animal exports for slaughter
- Impose stronger controls on bush meat

Chapter 8

Empowering, Educating and Protecting Our Communities

A vote for UKIP is a vote to give you the power to call binding referendums on local or national issues. It is a vote for safer, better-educated, vibrant and economically viable communities with good transport links and local councils that are run efficiently and cost-effectively. It is a vote for free and aspirational education for our children; investment in vocational training and apprenticeships and free tuition fees for the less well-off. It is a vote to end the 'developers' charter' and protect our precious greenbelt land.

Communities are the backbone of Britain. Wherever we live, we want to feel safe and have access to good housing, first-class education, effective health and social services, handy shops and sports facilities and efficient transport.

Sadly, what too many of us actually get, particularly in impoverished inner-city areas, is failing schools, overcrowded and ugly housing, potholed roads, fly-tipping, graffiti, boarded-up shops and high levels of crime and anti-social behaviour. How on earth did we let this happen in our supposedly civilised, first-world and wealthy country? And how are we going to reverse this decline?

Empowering communities to make a difference

Clearly, if we are to improve our communities, we cannot continue as we are at the moment. Today, our local communities are under attack: at a time when national government policies are putting increased and unsustainable pressure on councils, the government takes money away from them while continuing to give more and more in contributions to the EU, in the foreign aid budget, and in wasteful spending.

It often seems that politicians have forgotten they work for us. They – and the unelected bureaucrats who often tell the politicians what their policies should be – ignore or override the voice of the people, and instead of investing in the core services local people want and value, they ignore basic needs such as a weekly bin collection, while enforcing all manner of unwanted and costly schemes upon us.

Introduce binding national and local referendums

Because UKIP is passionate about both people power and engaging people in politics, one way in which we will seek to facilitate both is by introducing binding referendums on significant national or local issues. At the moment, local authorities can be forced to initiate a local referendum on council tax increases of over 3 per cent, but not on major planning projects that can completely change the character of their environment. In 2011 we were given a referendum on our voting system that no one really wanted except for Nick Clegg and his MPs, but we have been refused a referendum on the issues of staying in the EU or on gay marriage, both of which generate far more interest and arguably should have been subject to a plebiscite, whatever your personal views on either might be.

UKIP favours a process which gives local people the power to initiate a binding poll on any local issue with major implications; while national referendums would be a 'safety net' when the political class are out of touch with the public on serious issues such as, say, military action.

Not only would such a move force national and local government to 'look over its shoulder more often', as Nigel Farage has put it, it will also encourage real 'localism' and community engagement in issues that affect our neighbourhoods. It would deliver true localism which the Conservatives promised but never delivered; instead of giving people more of a say on planning matters, for instance, they actually stripped powers away.

The government's housing targets are a case in point. In rural and suburban neigbourhoods across the country local people are up in arms about precious green fields being turned into building sites to satisfy demand for new homes, of which the government says we need 200,000 a year.

This has effectively introduced a 'developers' charter'. Locals may object to new housing developments, but councillors usually roll over and pass the plans, advised by their officers that they will lose, expensively, on appeal if they refuse. Even if plans do get turned down by planning committees, the government nearly always over-turns their decisions on appeal because new housing targets come before the people already living in the area, and the government's 'reforms' of planning have cunningly created a legal environment which favours developers. In the interim, no one bothers to plan for the unaffordable new schools, doctor's surgeries, hospitals, roads, railway stations, bus routes, parks or shops that the inhabitants of the new houses will need, and so the critical shortage in public ser-vices continues apace and we become an ever-more over-crowded and under-resourced country. Meanwhile, the character of villages and small towns is destroyed forever.

In government, not only would UKIP reduce the demand for housing by ending EU open door immigration, providing incen-tives to reuse Britain's empty homes, directing new housing and business developments to brown field sites to protect the greenbelt and remove the right of appeal against local planning decisions on major developments, we would also give you the option of calling us to account using those binding referendums.

This facility is important not just because we believe in giving people more say in decision-making at a local and national level, but also because we want to restore faith and trust in a political system which has all but broken down.

Better connected communities

Although councils make millions out of motorists through fines and parking charges, local roads are often a disgrace. Road maintenance should be improved as a priority, with mending potholes taking precedence. Upgrading public transport systems, especially rural bus routes which many communities depend upon and which feed town centre businesses and markets, is a key policy for UKIP, as is reopening railway lines where they are needed to reinvigorate our communities. UKIP is also keen to see free parking in town centres to boost business, and at hospitals where, as already mentioned, charging is really just a tax on being sick.

Building safer communities

Many of Britain's communities suffer unacceptable levels of crime and anti-social behaviour, yet frontline policing jobs are being cut. UKIP would stop this and get more police out on our streets, not just to deter criminals but to help people feel safer. We know seeing policemen and women out and about helps reduce the fear of crime, which can be debilitating even to those who live in low-crime areas, let alone to those in crime-ridden neighbourhoods. To date, the police have been so over-burdened by serious crime, so short-staffed and time-bound by excessive form-filling, they have had little choice but to ignore anti-social behaviour, minor crime and problems with nuisance neighbours, for example. UKIP would free them from the burden of paperwork as well as investing in real policing, so we can insist they then take a zero-tolerance approach to anti-social behaviour and so-called 'petty' crime. This can be devastating and ruin lives and should not be overlooked or dismissed as unimportant.

UKIP also believes policing and the criminal justice system needs reforming to make sentences meaningful, rehabilitate offenders and deport foreign criminals. Victims rightly feel their pain has been ignored when prisoners are let out of jail early, and there are far too many horror stories in the press day after day about criminals who have committed serious crimes, are released early and then re-offend. UKIP believes sentences should mean what they say; in particular, we believe life should mean life.

The usual retort to this is that there are not enough prison spaces to accommodate such a move. UKIP will not allow this argument to force us into being soft on crime – it is time to start putting victims' rights first.

Statistics from the Ministry of Justice reveal that, as of 31 March 2013, there were 10,725 foreign nationals in prisons in England and Wales, a figure which represents 13 per cent of the total prison population. It is estimated that each new prison place costs £119,000 and that the annual average cost for each prisoner exceeds £40,000[87] – more than the cost of many good private boarding schools. This is unacceptable and must change. By leaving the EU, we can in the first place prevent known criminals from EU member states coming into the country, as well as those from elsewhere in the world, something we cannot do at the moment. UKIP will also deport all foreign criminals.

We will also remove ourselves from the jurisdiction of the European Court of Human Rights which too often prevents us from deporting criminals once they have served their sentences. In 2011–12

---

87 *The Economic Case For and Against Prison* by Kevin Marsh, Matrix Knowledge Group, 2009.

for instance, 409 appeals against deportations were allowed. Of these, 177 were allowed on the grounds of Article 8 of the European Convention on Human Rights – the right to respect for private and family life.[88]

The Human Rights Act has failed and has become a 'criminals' charter', protecting the wrongdoer at the expense of decent, law-abiding citizens. Now, we are told by Europe that we must give prisoners the vote and stop locking up even serial or mass murderers for life.

Much more needs to be done to prevent re-offending. At the moment, our prisons are frequently places where criminals simply learn how to become better criminals – according to the Ministry of Justice, re-offending rates with twelve months of release from prison were around 27 per cent in 2010/11. For criminals who use drugs, the rate rockets to over 57 per cent. Too often convicts have been let down by the education system; there is a staggeringly high percentage of criminals who cannot read or write. Over half of male offenders and over three-quarters of female offenders have no qualifications whatsoever when they enter prison,[89] and more than one in three people in prison have a reading level expected of an eleven-year-old.[90] Nearly half have been excluded from school[91] and most (67 per cent) were unemployed at the time of their imprisonment.[92] Yet less than a third of prisoners have access to prison education at any given time.[93]

We need to make sure prisons are places of learning, either academic or skills-based, and rehabilitation from addictions, so prisoners have a far better chance of making a new and law-abiding life for themselves on release. They must also be properly supported in their

---

88 Ministry of Justice figures.
89 HM Government, 'Reducing Reoffending Through Skills and Employment' (2005), p.6.
90 Home Office, 'Reducing Reoffending: National Action Plan' (2004), p.15.
91 Fatherhood Institute factsheet.
92 Department for Innovation, Universities and Skills, 'Skills for Life: Changing Lives' (2009), p.13.
93 House of Commons Education and Skills Committee, 2004 report.

new life once outside the prison walls – just clocking in with their probation officer is not good enough.

And if we still do not have enough prison places having made all these reforms? Then we will build more. It is not rocket science, and however much we might regret the circumstances which lead someone into a life of crime and want to give them a better chance on release, the first duty of any government must be to keep the people of their nation safe.

A better future for our children

Education should be about giving our children the best possible start in life and doing the best we can by each individual child, according to their needs. Instead, education has become highly politicised: government after government has experimented with different systems, teaching and learning methods, clutching onto the latest educational craze, and our children, instead of being put first, have been treated as pawns in a political game.

Teachers have also been let down. They do one of the most valuable and significant jobs it is possible to do, yet they too fall victim to the latest government target or scheme and often find themselves overburdened with paperwork and red tape, struggling to keep up with the latest changes and demands of this policy or that policy. After decades of having been discouraged from applying discipline, they can even feel at risk in their own classrooms, either from unruly children or, perhaps worse, from their unruly parents.

The policy of successive recent governments has also been to oppose competitiveness in schools, meaning the brightest or ablest children are not challenged and encouraged to realise their full potential. It is 'politically correct' to treat children as though they are all the same, when of course they quite clearly are not. Some have academic capabilities and will thrive in the academic arena; others will flourish in a different way, with a particular skill or talent, which needs to be nurtured and maximised so they can make a happy and fulfilled life for themselves. This is why UKIP favours a return to the selective grammar school system, within a multifaceted secondary education system which places a renewed focus on technical and vocational training and apprenticeships.

In praise of the grammar school

UKIP is in favour of grammar schools because they give bright kids from poorer backgrounds whose parents cannot afford private school fees access to a high standard of education that challenges them academically and encourages them to be the best they can be. And they work. But that does not matter to most Labour and Lib Dem MPs, who would like to see the few remaining grammars closed down; or to the Tories, who refuse to allow any new grammar schools to open, despite this being possible in certain areas under current legislation, and despite the fact that a majority of the general population – and especially Conservative voters – want them. In a 2010 ICM poll for the National Grammar Schools Association for instance, 76 per cent of adults and 85 per cent of those eighteen to twenty-four said they supported the introduction of new state grammar schools, especially in urban areas where there currently are none.[94] A You-Gov poll of Greater London residents in June 2013[95] revealed that 66 per cent of Conservative voters agreed the government should encourage more schools to select by academic ability, and build more grammar schools.

Once again though, politicians refuse to listen. Labour's hypocrisy is astonishing: obsessed to the point of madness with 'equality', the 'class system', and anything that seems even remotely 'hierarchical', even socialist MPs who benefitted from grammar schools now turn their backs on them because they cannot abide 'selection'. Yet

94   ICM poll, 15 February 2010.
95   YouGov/*Sunday Times* survey, 2010.

what is the current comprehensive system but 'selection' of a difference kind – selection by house price? The good schools are those in wealthier areas where richer parents can afford to buy properties near good schools, and are more likely to take an active interest in a schools' performance. The poor kids, deprived of any opportunity of getting a decent education, are just kept poor.

There is one good argument against grammar schools, one which says children are 'written off' by a single examination aged eleven, and then never get a second chance at a good academic education. This is absolutely right: some children do slip through the net for all manner of reasons, which is why UKIP would update the grammar system to offer children who initially failed their original selection exam but showed subsequent academic promise the chance to gain a place at a later date.

For the old party politicians though, the argument is not about what is best for children, it is about social engineering. Every single member of the current education team in David Cameron's Cabinet has been privately educated, as has the Labour Party's shadow Education Minister Tristram Hunt. It is absolutely typical of the political class to deny to others what they themselves have benefitted from, in this case a first-class education.

Focusing on skills and apprenticeships

UKIP has long made the case that vocational training and apprenticeships are vital if we are to deal with the skills shortage in our country.

'Many employers complain that not enough of our young people have the skills they require, while many youngsters are left on the scrap heap with little prospect of getting on,' says Margot Parker MEP.

Employers are, sadly, increasingly turning to a foreign work force instead of focusing on training young British people, and this is damaging the prospects of many young people in Britain. Youth unemployment in this country is still running at around one million, a shocking situation that we must solve by getting many more youngsters into the workforce.

UKIP believes we must ensure that those who are not academic can access quality vocational education and apprenticeships, enabling them to enter the workforce when they leave school and then progress through their careers from a practical, sporting or creative, rather than academic, starting point. Trying to force young people into academic routes when they are not suited to them is pointless; this is why UKIP will also reverse Tony Blair's targets for enforcing ever-wider participation in higher education.

No university targets and fairer tuition fees

In 2002, Tony Blair's Labour government set a target that at least half of all of young people should enter higher education. Eight years later, the Association of Graduate Recruiters was calling for the target to be scrapped on the grounds that it did nothing for standards and only devalued degrees. UKIP agreed – the target was utterly futile, except for massaging unemployment figures, and created a generation of young people mired in debt and unable to find work.

UKIP believes that whether or not to continue in higher education is a choice that should be made freely and independently and not because of any external pressures. Nonetheless, we will do all we can to support young people who do wish to go to university, and this includes looking at how we can cut tuition fees.

UKIP believes the dramatic increase in tuition fees is a scandal, as are the giant student loans that graduates now find themselves burdened with. Both penalise all children, and in particular less well-off children who are far more likely to be deterred from going to University, for example, because of the fear of getting into debt. While the current economic climate does not support the abolition of tuition fees, a UKIP government will ensure that no tuition fees are paid by young adults from a low-to-middle-income family on approved degree courses that are helping fill Britain's skills' gap. UKIP would also reintroduce a system of grants, not loans, for those least able to afford to pay, and who choose occupational degrees that are likely to lead to a future job.

In a nutshell, the vision UKIP has for education in Britain is of schooling that reflects a pupil's ability, whether that be academic or skills-based, enables them to learn in an environment that suits them, encourages them to be the best they can be, reduces the likelihood of them being unemployed, and empowers Britain to compete in a global market.

Vote UKIP to:

- Guarantee binding referendums on local and national issues
- Empower communities
- End the 'developers' charter'
- Protect the greenbelt
- Maintain roads properly
- Improve public transport
- Invest in high-quality state education, including grammar schools
- Promote vocational and skills-based training
- Encourage apprenticeships
- End the 50 per cent higher education target
- Abolish tuition fees and student loans for those from low-to-middle-income families on approved courses that are helping fill the UK skills' gap

Chapter 9

Taking Pride in Britain

A vote for UKIP is a vote to embrace patriotic British values, to uphold the supremacy of British law, to free public services from the tyranny of the political philosophy of multiculturalism and, in a nutshell, start taking pride in our nation again.

Britain is a vibrant and beautiful country and gives us much to be proud of. We are the envy of the world for our rich history, our art and architecture, our literary heritage, our monarchy, world-famous brands like the BBC, the fact we invented parliamentary democracy and football. We led the way in the abolition of the slave trade; we shaped the industrial revolution; Great Britons discovered gravity, penicillin, the world wide web, the steam engine and the jet engine, the structure of DNA; Britain is the home of The Beatles, Charlie Chaplin, Shakespeare, Miss Marple, James Bond and Harry Potter.

What a fantastic country! So why do so many of us turn our noses up at the word 'patriotism', and why do we get to sing our national anthem less and less, if at all? When did we start to knock Britain? When did it become unfashionable to say you were proud to be British?

Standing up for Britain

Britain was once a strong and great nation – an empire that ruled half the world. We knew where we stood in the grand scheme of things and had complete confidence in our sovereignty. Everyone shared a strong sense of patriotism; we led the way in industry, in commerce, in law. We had a unique and influential role in shaping the modern world and we knew it. We had self-belief.

Now we seem to be having something of an identity crisis. Some have called it 'post-colonial guilt'; the idea that because we dared to have an empire in the past, we now have to atone for our 'sins'; that we have no right to feel proud of a once powerful nation that ruled half the world, even though we have given the vast majority of it back, with democratic and judicial dividends attached.

This pressure to do ourselves down was symbolised in 2007 at the time of the 200th anniversary of the abolition of the slave trade, a time you might think, when we might have applauded the role Britain played in bringing it to an end. Oh no. Instead, events were dominated by calls for Tony Blair to make a formal apology for Britain's role in the slave trade, on behalf of the whole country, despite the fact he had absolutely nothing whatsoever to do with it and neither, of course, did anyone else alive. Presumably whoever is Prime Minister in 2057, on the 250th anniversary, will have to apologise all over again.

Blair was being called to apologise for still being British. There has also been a growing call for 'compensation' to be paid to countries that consider themselves to have a grievance against our forebears. But we cannot change what is now ancient history, so why should we? Where would it end and what good would it do if every country in the world was being continually asked to apologise for its past? Surely it is where we go from here that is important?

UKIP believes it is good to be British and that there is nothing wrong with a benign patriotism which has for too long been the subject of smear and ridicule. UKIP also believes it is fine, if you want to, to cherish the ideas and institutions which were once at the heart of British life and which protected British values, but which are now denigrated and dismissed as old-fashioned: the monarchy, the Church, the traditional family, the rule of law, good manners and keeping a 'stiff upper lip' etc. These are regularly berated, mostly by left-wing social scientists and columnists: you can almost hear the sneer of contempt by the socialist intelligentsia when people line the streets waving little flags and host street parties to celebrate momentous royal events like Prince William's marriage and the Queen's golden jubilee. Thankfully though, most of us still feel a sense of pride when Britain puts on a show of great pageantry and tradition and the more of us who can stand up to the doomsayers and the would-be republicans, the better.

Not that championing what Britain does best and standing up to these types is easy. Witness, for example, what happened when David Cameron told the *Church Times* that Christians should be 'confident' in standing up to defend their values and their faith. Before you could say a single Hail Mary, fifty mostly left-wing atheists had penned a letter to *The Times* saying that while they respected the Prime Minister's right to his own religious beliefs, 'We object to his characterisation of Britain as a "Christian country" and the negative consequences for politics and society that this engenders.'

Hang on a minute – the Queen is Head of State and Head of the Church of England. Surely that means Britain still *is* a Christian country, in principle, at least, even if not in practice? Why get so upset about it? And how can Christian principles in any case have 'negative' consequences when, like it or not, they already underpin our laws and our concepts of democracy and equality? Whether you like it or not, and whether you attend or not, there is no doubt that the Church plays a positive, vibrant and vital role in our schools, our communities and in wider society, and in the grand scheme of things – today at least – does very little harm.

Arguably, it is the denigration of Christianity and Christian values in the public realm that has had negative consequences for society; that bowing down to 'political correctness' such as this has turned us into a nation of people too scared to say what we think, for fear of upsetting someone. Would Cameron have come under the same fire if he had said Buddhists, or Zoroastrians, or Hindus should feel confident in standing up for their faith? It seems unlikely. But these faiths are not intrinsically 'British' so perhaps that is why we do not have to apologise for talking about them. The Church, on the other hand, presumably 'conspired' with the colonialists, so Christianity, generations later, must fall over backwards apologising for itself and must not expect any preferential treatment in the public realm, despite still being the official state religion. By saying it was tolerable for Cameron to hold a faith position privately, but that he should shut up about his beliefs in public, the fifty who wrote to *The Times* rather neatly illustrated this point.

The tyranny of multiculturalism

Meanwhile, the same aggressive and secular left-wing that loathes Christianity promotes 'multiculturalism', an authoritarian philosophy of social engineering that paradoxically, given its name, will not tolerate alternative viewpoints and has had the depressing effect of dividing Britain into many different race, faith and cultural groups, creating independent, isolationist, segregated, and often competing communities.

Multiculturalism in the UK welcomes open door immigration, believing that cultural, religious and racial diversity can only ever enrich Britain, so the more multicultural and the less 'British' we become, the better. Multiculturalism dictates that any attempt to get non-white, non-Christian, non-British individuals or communities to integrate into the host culture is colonial or cultural imperialism and should be shunned; instead newcomers should be encouraged to continue the customs, practices and languages of their place of origin. Significantly, multiculturalism preaches that all cultures, races and religions are morally positive and that no one culture, race or religion should ever be considered 'superior' in any way to any other. So, patriotism is outlawed on the basis it breeds racism and discrimination. The idea that a set of over-arching British (and, God forbid, Christian) values, together with a common language (English) could be employed in a positive way, to unite all cultures in a rich, harmonious and integrated diversity is utterly abhorrent to the multiculturalist. Multiculturalism aims to ensure that there will never be a 'dominant' culture; to that end, the culture of the majority must be done away with.

Promoted zealously by the Labour government from 1997 to 2010, alongside a deliberate policy of mass immigration to hurry it along, multiculturalism has been a disaster for Britain. It has created a many-headed monster that few dare fight, because its gaze has hypnotised us, enslaved us and paralysed us with fear.

Its main victims have been women and children whose rights under the law have been trampled by its pernicious hold over us. It has kept them in chains to outdated, violent cultural practices that have no place in Britain and should not be tolerated: so-called 'honour' crimes, female genital mutilation (FGM), forced, underage and sham marriages, Asian grooming gangs, child 'witchcraft' abuse – all serious and, astonishingly, growing problems in Britain. Why were these appalling practices allowed to proliferate? Because the special privileges afforded under equalities legislation to the ethnic minority communities that practise these horrendous crimes paralyse the police, social workers, teachers – anyone in a position to challenge them. Why? Because multiculturalism rules anyone suggesting certain communities or individuals are somehow less civilised or criminal because of their cultural background is racist and should lose their job.

Now this *is* something Britain should be ashamed of: our failure to give the same hard-won freedom and protection under the law to women and children in the black and Asian communities that we take for granted for white people and, worse, to have been so brainwashed by the loony left that we believed we were doing it 'in their best interests'.

Multiculturalism has also provided fertile ground in which extremism can breed: we have allowed Islamic 'courts' to operate freely in Britain, to dish out informal community justice without asserting the primacy of British law and making it clear to participants that their judgements are not binding in Britain. We have allowed book burnings and flag burnings and brutal demonstrations that threaten death to those with a different view of literature or cartoons to escape arrest, so the rule of British law appears even more feeble. Widespread anti-Semitism, homophobia and the unequal treatment of women has been ignored by hypocritical politicians who have a duty to condemn such behaviour outright but turn a blind eye because they want the ethnic vote. We have welcomed into Britain and given homes and welfare payments to hate preachers who corrupt and radicalise young people in our communities, young people who care so little about Britain – having never been encourage to feel pride in their own country – that they are prepared to go and fight in Syria and Iraq under the banner of an Islamic terrorist organisation.

This is the legacy of multiculturalism and it is a right mess. There are no quick fixes and no easy answers when it comes to sorting it out.

Reverse multiculturalism

If multiculturalism, and accepting an 'anything goes' attitude, caused the problem, will a kind of 'reverse multiculturalism' help solve it? Certainly it is UKIP's view that the only way we can start to integrate our communities again is by turning our backs on multiculturalism and working to bring people together as a united whole, under the banner of Britishness.

Says UKIP's culture spokesman, Peter Whittle:

We need to work towards reinvigorating civic life at a local level, restoring a sense of civic pride and involvement among local communities, and recognising and valuing an overarching, unifying British culture, which is inclusive and open to anyone who wishes to identify with Britain and British values, regardless of their ethnic or religious background.

Central to this for Whittle is the prominence of the English language, and now, thankfully, it is acceptable to say newcomers to the country should learn English, a view that was once frowned upon. UKIP would also end the use of divisive multi-lingual formatting on official application forms at a local and national level while respecting Welsh, Gaelic, Cornish and other indigenous languages.

It is also about how we educate children and young people about Britain and undoing the damage that has been done by an education system that has focused more on changing society and trying to engineer freedom, justice and 'equality' rather than explaining how we won it historically, how hard Britain has fought for it and why therefore it is of paramount importance.

A UKIP government would also take a zero-tolerance approach to practices which are illegal under British law, such as forced marriages, FGM and so-called 'honour killings'. Says Whittle:

> The onus is also on us to make clear what is and is not acceptable in British culture. Not only should it be stated loud and clear that such practices (which, while hiding under the cloak of religion, are mostly purely cultural ones) are an affront to all notions of decency and basic morality. It should be made clear from the highest points in our society that they are utterly incompatible with our values, and will in no circumstances be tolerated. They should be eradicated completely.[96]

Crucially, UKIP would ensure no public money is paid to any public body which promotes divisiveness or advocates tolerating the intolerable through policies of enforced public multiculturalism. If we want to repair our society, we have to believe in the values generations

96 *Being British: What's Wrong With It?* by Peter Whittle, Biteback Publishing, 2012.

have fought and died for, not simply chuck them into the melting pot as a less than favourable option.

Does any of this offend you? Well, we all have the right to be offended, there is no law that says we don't, and in the English language, offence is not 'given' but 'taken' and perhaps too many of us take it far too quickly nowadays. As Peter Whittle says:

> It is exasperating and morale-sapping to always be walking on egg shells ... The whining over offence, and the huge emphasis put on the need to publicly apologise for real or imagined slights is a sign of an infantilised society, one which needs to be constantly stroked and placated. We must start treating each other, whether individuals or groups, as adults again.

As UKIP's mission statement says: 'We believe that the nation can be a force for good, that patriotism is a virtue, and that our country has developed social and civic values over a thousand years which should be celebrated, preserved and built upon.'

Amen to that.

Vote UKIP to:

- Restore a sense of pride in Britain and in British values and culture
- Uphold the supremacy of British law above any other form of law
- End support and funding for multiculturalism
- Take a zero-tolerance approach to cruel and outdated cultural practices
- Teach Britain's achievements and influence in shaping the modern world in our schools
- End multi-lingual formatting on official forms and other documents

Chapter 10

UKIP in Government

A vote for UKIP is a vote for a government that will clean up Westminster and never forget that politicians are the servants of the people – not the other way around. It is a vote for a government that will give voters real power of recall to get rid of MPs who fiddle their expenses or profit from excessive lobbying practices; for a smaller and more democratic government; for tackling fake 'political' charities. A UKIP government will light a bonfire of the quangos, cut expensive 'special advisors' and make 'government tsars' more accountable.

'We will act rapidly to push through far-reaching reforms to restore ethics to politics and revive the electorate's faith in politicians [and] introduce a power of recall to allow electors to kick out MPs, a power that will be triggered by proven serious wrongdoing.'

These were promises made in the Conservative Party manifesto of 2010.[97] What actually happened? Not a lot. The 'cash for peerages' row continues unabated as parties reward rich donors with titles. Lib Dem Mike Hancock MP still clings to his Westminster seat despite admitting to acting inappropriately towards a vulnerable woman and numerous calls for him to quit. It took David Cameron six days to sack Maria Miller MP from her Cabinet post after she was told to repay £5,800 of expenses she had claimed for a second

---

97 'Invitation to Join the Government of Britain: The Conservative Party Manifesto 2010', p.65–6.

home in which her parents were living (the independent parliamentary commissioner for standards had previously recommended she repay £45,000). Mr Cameron immediately said he hoped she would return to the Cabinet 'in due course'. It almost seems unfair to single out Ms Miller and Mr Hancock however, given the numerous peccadillos of many other MPs in all parties who have also had to pay back expenses or, while not engaging in any actual rule-breaking, have pushed the limits of acceptability by making claims for second home allowances in the capital for instance, despite already owning other properties they could, or actually do, live in that are so close to town they could easily commute like the rest of us.

What of the promise of recall? The issue has been completely fudged. Under legislation proposed in the Queen's speech, constituents can only sack their MP if they have been sentenced to up to twelve months in jail and the actual power of recall is in the power of a group of MPs, which rather defeats the object of having a recall in the first place – forget being able to 'kick out' your corrupt, lazy or fraudulent MP; unless you can get other MPs to break ranks, you are stuck with them.

The LibLabCon have talked for decades about cleaning up politics and giving more power back to the people, but when push comes to shove, they just cannot bring themselves to do it. It is time to let UKIP get on with the job for them, to remind the political class that they are public servants and introduce a proper power of recall for MPs which puts that power in the hands of the people.

Smaller, more democratic government

UKIP believes the government which is best is the government which governs least. Currently, government interferes far too much in our lives and has become unnecessarily huge and expensive.

In the summer of 1940, when Britain was facing its greatest crisis in history at the outset of the Second World War, the government had nine Cabinet ministers. There are now twenty-two secretaries of state and eighty-seven ministers or parliamentary under-secretaries of state. Can they really all be necessary, especially given the amount of legislation and areas of control for which the EU takes responsibility?

The departments they all run have proliferated too and UKIP believes Whitehall has at least six major spending departments that the British taxpayer would not miss too much, most of them created in the Blair/Brown years. The Department for International Development, the Ministry of Justice, the Department of Energy and Climate Change, the Department for Communities and Local Government, the Department for Culture, Media and Sport and the Department for Business, Innovation and Skills are all either relatively new departments or departments whose responsibilities previously came under the auspices of others. We survived for decades without these departments and they cost us billions. UKIP would at the very least scale them back, keeping only their essential functions, such as nuclear decommissioning in the Department of Energy and Climate Change for example.

Once in Parliament, UKIP would also shine a light into the dark world of the numerous quangos, 'SPADs', 'government tsars' and 'fake charities' that operate in and around Westminster at the taxpayers' expense, despite being unaccountable to the electorate.

Lighting a bonfire of the quangos

Quangos, 'quasi-autonomous non-governmental organisations', are arm's-length bodies funded by Whitehall departments but not run by them. Supposedly independent advisory bodies, consumer watchdogs and organisations carrying out public services, they are created by government to deliver policy, offer expertise and oversee regulation, among other tasks. There are an awful lot of them, they cost an exceedingly large fortune yet are undemocratic, bureaucratic, and enable politicians to 'pass the buck'. Many of them duplicate the work of others and UKIP believes many of them could go.

When Tony Blair's government came into power there were 859 quangos. He promised to get rid of them but he must have found they worked to his advantage, because an investigation by the *Daily Telegraph* found that over the first decade of his administration, the number of quangos actually soared to more than two and a half thousand, an increase of 41 per cent, and the cost of running them rose to a staggering £123.8 billion.[98] They were a marvellous jolly for freeloading old cronies: by the time Labour left office in 2010, it was revealed 77 per cent of those appointed to quangos who declared a political background were Labour supporters. Still, under John Major's Conservative government 57 per cent had been Conservative.[99] Funny that. So much for their supposed 'independence'.

UKIP's Head of Policy, Tim Aker, recalls:

> In opposition to Labour, the Conservative Party criticised the growth of the quango and pledged root and branch reform. However, once they arrived in power in 2010, that policy was quickly derailed by the need to keep sinecures available for friends and supporters. Their programme of reform rather resembled the shell-game, with some distinctly original accounting involved.

So far, the coalition has only abolished some 200 quangos and created a handful more. A UKIP government will finish the job and put accountability back where it belongs: in the hands of elected MPs, not unelected 'chums' of politicians who can toe the party line while taking home large salaries.

---

98 As reported by Dan Hodges in the *Daily Telegraph*, 2 February 2014.
99 Data released by the Commissioner for Public Appointments.

SPADs in spades: time to end 'jobs for the boys'

The plethora of 'special advisors' to ministers, commonly known as 'SPADs' in and around Westminster, are another group earmarked for extinction – or at least a cull – by UKIP. Often they are little more than assorted 'hangers on', but rather grand ones – they can be paid up to £142,668 per annum by central government despite being party political appointments. They also get a coveted parliamentary pass. SPADs cost the government in the region of £7.2 million each year[100] yet they are shadowy figures whose names are rarely known outside Whitehall. Often they are very young with little work or life experience, they have no training for their roles and they are not accountable to anyone except their ministers. Their posts are never advertised, despite the fact they are clearly a stepping-stone into top jobs in politics.

SPADs are frequently wannabe MPs who use the positions to get their first foot into the door of parliament (Ed Balls and both Miliband brothers are former special advisors). Those who fail to make it onto either the green or red benches often go on to find lucrative posts in the private sector – or on quangos – thanks to their close links to the corridors of power.

Again, the LibLabCon have promised in the past to stop this abuse. In 2009 Nick Clegg criticised the number and increase of SPADs in the Labour government and the cost, then, of £5.9 million each year. 'These are political jobs and they should be paid for by political parties,' said a 2009 Lib Dem policy paper. A month after he became Deputy Prime Minister, he himself took on four SPADs and despite his earlier rhetoric, now employs fifteen. At the last count there were ninety-eight SPADs out of a total 447,000 established civil servants, costing £7.2 million.

UKIP believes if nothing else SPADs should be completely transparent in their dealings, their job roles should be clearly defined,

---

100 Hansard, 19 Nov 2013: Column 1068.

and we should know who else they may work for, or for whom they are lobbying behind the scenes.

Tackling 'fake' political charities

When any charity relies upon the government for a significant portion of its funding, questions must surely be asked about its neutrality. Is it really a charity or a 'fake charity' which is really part of the state?

Charities are supposedly banned under charity law from engaging in political campaigning yet this is rarely enforced, not least because there are so many grey areas. UKIP's immediate concern is with the use of taxpayers' money when it is paid over to charities who are involved in lobbying for change to pursue a political agenda, whether or not it is aligned with the agenda of the government of the day.

Chris Snowdon summed the situation up is his 2012 report: 'Sock Puppets: How the Government Lobbies Itself and Why'. He cited charities such as the Fawcett Society, Living Streets, Child Poverty Action Group, War on Want and Oxfam to illustrate the variety of causes pursued by charities that receive significant chunks of their income from government sources. When he wrote the report, 27,000 charities in total were dependent on the government for at least three-quarters of their income.

Clearly, there is nothing wrong with government paying the voluntary sector to carry out specific humanitarian or service tasks which individual charities may be well-qualified to do and which are cost-effective to the state, so everyone benefits. UKIP has no issue with this, nor with any of the above listed charities which may be working in this way. The problem is when taxpayer-funded charities engage in political activity. The National Association for Voluntary and Community Action, for instance, states on its website its aim to 'influence national and local government policy' (although on the charities' register the wording is 'make sure policy makers understand

the needs of local voluntary organisations and community groups').
NAVCA relies on grants from the Department for Education, the
Home Office, the Office for Civil Society, the Ministry of Justice, the
Department of Health and the Lottery Fund for most of its income.

'Lobbying government' is not a role taxpayers recognise as being
charitable and their money should not be used for it. UKIP will bring
this practice to an end both for this reason and because there is a huge
question mark over whether or not government might be funding
charities to come up with the conclusions they want to reach with
regard to particular issues, which they can then use to sanction policy.

The European Union is a past master at this. As we have already
seen, the EU is a passionate advocate of the 'green' agenda. To justify and promote its policies it clearly needs 'evidence'. It gets this
evidence from numerous 'green' charities, to which it pays huge
grants. It is effectively shelling out millions of euros to green activ-
ists to lobby itself.

In the past sixteen years, the EU has handed over more than £90
million to green groups.[101] These include the World Wide Fund for
Nature (£7.4 million) and Friends of the Earth Europe (£6.4 million)
which, among other activities, produced a video which lobbied the
British and German governments to back an EC energy savings directive which has since come into force.

According to Friends of the Earth Europe, the charity received half
of its total annual funding in 2012 from at least seven different departments of the European Commission so, the taxpayer shells out twice:
first for the expensive grants and then by way of larger fuel bills as a
result of the measures put in place as a result of successful lobbying.

Matthew Sinclair, the chief executive of the TaxPayers' Alliance at
the time, said: 'The funding is an unfair subsidy on behalf of many
people who may not agree with the environmentalist campaigners'
objectives, and biases European environmental policy.'[102]

---

101 Analysis by the Institute of Economic Affairs.
102 'European Union funding £90 million green lobbying con', *Daily Telegraph*, 21 December 2013.

UKIP agrees: Brussels has no right squandering our money in this way and neither should any government be financing charities to the point where their independence risks being compromised.

Government tsars – either make them accountable or ditch them

The use of so-called government 'tsars' has exploded in recent years: a report by King's College, London, found that over 260 tsars were appointed between May 1997 and July 2012. The authors also found the prominence of tsars has soared, from a rate of three appointments per annum in the first New Labour administration to a rate of forty-three per annum since the coalition came to power in 2010.[103]

They are often first hired when government faces calls to 'do something' about major social issues – knife crime, drug abuse, the demise of the High Street etc. The appointment of a 'tsar' – often a high-profile celebrity or known professional – subdues the clamour and unrest, at least temporarily.

But what exactly do they do? And are they really up to the job? It has been said they are, like SPADs, just another example of 'jobs for the boys' and quite literally in most cases: 85 per cent are male, 98 per cent are white, 71 per cent are aged over fifty and 38 per cent have titles. Hardly a diverse bunch.

Although called 'tsars' in the press, their actual titles are usually 'advisor', 'advocate', 'ambassador', 'commissioner', 'envoy' or, most commonly, 'reviewer'. Proper records of their actions are not kept, departmental reports rarely note any progress they have made or not. Some never even produce a written report and we have no idea whether or not they are briefing ministers in any other ways. Rarely have Select Committees in either House called them in.

Tsars do fail. It was recently reported that two years after Mary

---

103 By Dr Ruth Levitt and William Solesbury, Visiting Senior Research Fellows in the Department of Political Economy at King's College, London.

'Queen of Shops' Portas was hired by the government to turn around struggling towns, there are fifty-two fewer shops in twelve pilot areas than when she started the job, although to be fair, the government did not adopt some of her ideas, such as free parking.

The King's College authors concluded: 'Our review reveals a picture of ambiguity around the whole framework of the policy tsar. There is no consistency in just about every variable of tsars' appointments and outputs – from working hours to pay, reporting expectations and style of conduct.'

Tsars remain unregulated, unaccountable, and subject to no code of practice. Yet these are public appointments, publically financed and, in UKIP's view, either they should be accountable to parliament or their posts should be scrapped, if nothing else than to reassure us that their appointments really are important, and not just PR stunts to get ministers out of trouble when their backs are up against the wall.

This is what UKIP in government will look like: democratic, cost-effective, accountable, and a servant of the people.

Vote UKIP to:

- Clean up Westminster
- Give the public the power to recall their MPs
- Cut the size and expense of governmental departments
- Get rid of unnecessary quangos
- Cut the numbers of special advisors and shine a light on their activities
- Make sure charity is charitable, not political
- Insist 'tsars' are accountable

Conclusion

So there you have it, a whole set of reasons to vote UKIP.

If nothing else, in voting for UKIP you will be voting for a party that knows exactly where it stands on the issues of the day. No flannel, no waffle, no equivocation; no *volte-face* on important principles, and definitely no panicking when we think we might be losing ground to another party. UKIP just gets on with doing the job and does what it believes to be right.

Over the past twenty years, UKIP has stood firm when all others around have ridiculed, attacked and then finally copied Nigel Farage's 'people's army' policies. Barely a day goes by now when the Tory, Labour or Lib Dem leaders do not make some kind of announcement which is clearly a sop to UKIP voters, borne not out of common sense, or a genuine change of heart, but out of sheer desperation to get 'kippers' to change their vote.

Cameron announces a crackdown on migrant benefits, but forgets to mention his plans are illegal while we remain in the EU. Nick Clegg, after decades of campaigning for open-door migration and an amnesty for illegal immigrants, suddenly says he thinks EU migration needs to be cut. And Ed Miliband? Well, even Labour's own former communications chief admits his policies do not stand up to scrutiny and calls them a 'great steaming pile of fudge'.

Don't be fooled. Don't vote for a carbon copy party that will say anything to stay in or achieve power. Vote for the original. Vote UKIP.

Acknowledgements

UKIP chairman Steve Crowther was invaluable in going through my text, spotting any errors and suggesting amendments, and Tim Aker MEP, UKIP's policy guru, has been a godsend. I would also like to mention how helpful my amazing daughter was and how grateful I am to Biteback for giving me the opportunity to write this book.

A big thank you to you all.

About the Author

Suzanne Evans is deputy chairman of UKIP. A former councillor in the London Borough of Merton, she has represented UKIP on numerous TV and radio programmes, including *Question Time*, *Newsnight*, *Daily Politics*, *Murnaghan*, and the Radio 4 *Today* programme.

She is the prospective parliamentary candidate for UKIP in the Shrewsbury & Atcham constituency where she was born and grew up.

Previously a broadcaster and journalist, Suzanne now works freelance as a PR and marketing consultant. She founded the national health charity Lipoedema UK in 2011.

Also available from Biteback Publishing

THE POLITICOS GUIDE TO THE 2015 GENERAL ELECTION

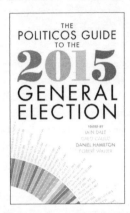

EDITED BY IAIN DALE, GREG CALLUS, DANIEL HAMILTON & ROBERT WALLER

The essential guide to the most eagerly awaited general election in recent history. Here, in one volume, is everything you need to make up your mind in the 2015 general election. This is a unique guide to the state of the parties, policies and issues in the run-up to next May's polling, including expert predictions from political pundits.

With its unique guide to the key marginal constituencies that will make up the battleground, expert commentary and comprehensive opinion poll analysis, this book will arm you with all the facts and figures you need to make an informed choice at the ballot box.

It also features lists of prospective candidates, examples of historical precedent, analysis of the key marginal seats and a comprehensive assessment of the political landscape as the country moves onto an election footing.

464pp paperback, £19.99

Available from all good bookshops
www.bitebackpublishing.com